THE VICTORIA & ALBERT MUSEUM'S
TEXTILE COLLECTION
WOVEN TEXTILE DESIGN IN BRITAIN TO 1750

THE VICTORIA & ALBERT MUSEUM'S TEXTILE COLLECTION

WOVEN TEXTILE DESIGN IN BRITAIN TO 1750

By Natalie Rothstein

CANOPY BOOKS
A DIVISION OF ABBEVILLE PUBLISHING GROUP
NEW YORK   LONDON   PARIS

First published in the United States of America in 1994
by Canopy Books, a Division of Abbeville Publishing Group,
488 Madison Avenue, New York, NY 10022.

First Published in Great Britain in 1994 by the Victoria &
Albert Museum, Cromwell Road, London SW7.

Printed and bound in Italy.

ISBN 1-55859-849-9

Designed by Area, London.

FRONT AND BACK COVER: Woven silk. Spitalfields, about 1707-08. 711-1864

Contents

ACKNOWLEDGMENTS

Thanks are extended to Mr Donald King, the former Keeper of the Textiles Department and editor of the original edition (1980) of the three volumes *British Textile Design in the Victoria and Albert Museum* and to Mr Takahiko Sano who performed amazing feats as photographer, editorial advisor and translator of the first series. Publications are dependent upon team efforts and many curators, past and present, of the Textiles and Dress Collection helped in the preparation of these books. Special mention must be made of the invaluable contribution made by Mrs Monique King whose expertise ensured the successful outcome of the project. That they are now re-issued for a wider audience is due to the thoughtfulness of the publishers Gakken, Tokyo; the support of Jennifer Blain and Lesley Burton of V&A Publishing and the diligence of Clare Woodthorpe Browne of Textiles and Dress.

Natalie Rothstein's continuing research into eighteenth century textiles and the English silk industry has resulted in two further major publications, *Barbara Johnson's Album of Fashions and Fabrics* (1987) and *Silk Designs of the Eighteenth Century in the Collection of the Victoria and Albert Museum* (1990). The latter accompanied an important exhibition *Flowered Silks: A Noble Manufacture of the Eighteenth Century* held at the Victoria and Albert Museum.

Valerie D Mendes
Curator, Textiles and Dress Collection

Woven Textile Design
in Britain to 1750

Natalie Rothstein

English Silks

Introduction

Sir Nicholas Pevsner wrote that no other European nation had "so abject an inferiority complex about its own aesthetic capabilities as England"[1] and this has certainly been very true of English attitudes to the decorative arts. Yet by the middle of the 18th century a French designer was forced to acknowledge that English silks were reaching foreign markets and that certain mediocre designers were established in England[2]. Another French critic was even more damning, both about the design and the quality of English silks[3]. The Customs figures in the period show a steady and sometimes even a dramatic rise in exports[4]. So were French critics worried about competition or being quite objective?

Some English commentators were entirely satisfied, not to say smug, denying any debt to France in the designs of English silks, albeit attributing some of English success to Huguenot refugees and mentioning a designer named Baudouin. Postlethwayt thought the silk designer and naturalist Joseph Dandridge "far superior" to the French and he considered English silks to be better in quality as well as design. "The designs of the French have a poverty and embarrassment in them, to say nothing of the constant repetition of the same objects which tire and offend the discerning eye"[5]. He said that the designs produced by Mrs. Anna Maria Garthwaite, Mr. John Vansommer and Mr. Peter Mazell succeeded in ten years in turning the taste of the English consumer from French to English silks. Whom should we believe?

The survival of work by most of the designers mentioned by Postlethwayt and other writers permits an assessment. Hogarth was a contemporary of many of those designers and his views on art are very relevant to them. In his *Analysis of Beauty* published in 1753 he extols the serpentine line – the Line of Beauty which he had drawn on the palette of his self-portrait in 1745. The essay on silk designing which appears in the 1756 edition of the *Laboratory or School of Arts* was wholly in agreement. The designer should "follow the principles Mr. Hogarth gives in his Analysis, observing the line of Beauty, so as to make it the foundation and support of all his designs, in ornaments, flowers, branches leafs etc."[6]. Already in November 1743 the designer Anna Maria Garthwaite had introduced it into her work (plate 119), nor can it be a coincidence that for his *Industrious and Idle Apprentice* of 1747 Hogarth chose – of all the trades in London – a pair of apprentice weavers in "Spittlefields". The silks and designs illustrated here may help us to see the qualities which Hogarth and others so admired. Can we also see how far English silks differed from their French contemporaries?

English silks, like other arts, participate aesthetically in the transformation from Baroque to Rococo. In Anglicising current styles, however, some distinctive trends can be observed. As Pevsner has pointed out when speaking of other forms of art, there is a preference for real as opposed to abstract objects, for colouring very close to nature and, perhaps more than anything else, for botanical naturalism whenever current aesthetic trends permitted this. Fuseli, quoted by Pevsner, when speaking of English artists said that "their taste and feeling go all to realities"[7]. Climate may certainly be a factor. The generic name for a drawloom woven silk in the period was "flowered" – and the inspiration was there almost all the year round. These preferences were combined with excellent technical quality which can be judged from the many surviving silks. Chemistry was already advanced by the 18th century and English dyers were consequently able to make consistent as well as beautiful colours. As a trading nation the British sent their silks, as a tiny but significant proportion of their exports, to all their normal markets. We may even ask whether these markets influenced patterns and the choice of colours produced for them. The survival of over a thousand designs from 1706 onwards and of a series of pattern books from the mid 18th century enables a more systematic analysis to be made of English silk design than of French[8]. The silks and designs for them illustrated here were produced, however, not for admiration by a later generation but as objects for sale. They had to meet the demands of fashion and the economics of price. They reflect public taste and public purchasing power.

THE SILK INDUSTRY

London was a textile centre, as it was also the chief manufacturing and exporting city for many other trades. The silk industry grew from a ribbon industry long established in the City. The Weavers Company, one of the oldest of the medieval guilds, adapted itself in the course of the 17th century to the numbers of 'Foreign Weavers' and 'Foreign Masters' it was asked to accept. Some of these Huguenot refugees came directly from France and some via Amsterdam and other cities. Few had been silk weavers in France[9], but their commercial acumen, their capital and their probity brought immense strength to the new broad silk industry which rapidly became established. The Revocation of the Edict of Nantes in 1685 temporarily checked the numbers but, thereafter, fugitives came secretly and adventurously to join friends and relatives already established. The majority of the silk industry from top to bottom were, however, always English. Only one pattern book of English silks from the 17th century survived and that was burnt at the Brussels exhibition of 1909. We cannot now judge, therefore, whether the English would have been able to substantiate their claim to be able to supply the Court. Surviving bills suggest that most silks of high fashion were imported either from France or, if they were furnishings, from Italy. Colbert's protectionist policy towards the Lyon silk industry had been enormously successful. By 1700 the London silk industry had begun to spread beyond the confines of the City down Bishopsgate Without to a district which was being newly developed called Spitalfields. As the industry expanded, so did the district[10]. Certain streets contained certain classes of master weavers; some came to be the homes of the richest and most important men in all the Branches of the industry – Spital Square, Princes Street, and Church Street – while others were inhabited by the middle rank of weavers. The journeymen who worked for them lived in the poorer streets or further away in hamlets like Bethnal Green and St. Dunstan's Stepney, coming to the master's warehouse to get their work and taking it away to weave at home. The industry was divided in Branches but without the formal regulations imposed in Lyon. The Foot-figured and Flowered Branch is the only one which concerns us here. By the middle of the century the weavers had become "as numerous as the names of the things they weave"[11] and these names were not ephemeral but represented important technical distinctions. Nearly the whole of the London output was, however, intended for dress and not furnishings, which naturally had a profound influence on their designs. There were a few important exceptions but, in general, not only was the demand for furnishing silk declining in favour of wallpapers and printed cottons during the 18th century, but such demand as did survive could be well met from the traditional sources in Italy.

Weavers specialised in one branch or another. Thus James Dalbiac made black silks. Three generations of the Lekeux family made the richest flowered silks, for example plates 69, 70. Lewis Chauvet made handkerchiefs. Simon Julins made various kinds of flowered silk at first, but came gradually to specialise in the weaving of damasks. Captain John Baker (he held the rank of Captain in the City Trained Bands, in which several men of Huguenot descent also held commissions), while producing flowered silks, made his money out of Ben Truman's brewery and the pubs he owned[12]. Unlike the French, the English industry was extremely flexible; throwsters became silkmen, rich weavers might buy their own silk and get it thrown, while poorer ones bought it ready thrown; some weavers sold for export, most sold to the mercers of Ludgate Hill and Covent Garden. Some weavers could produce a range of goods as a speculation and hope for mercers to place orders while, increasingly, most began to work to commission from the mercers. There were no partnerships between weavers and mercers and most of the journeymen worked independently on piece-work – but some families worked for forty years or more for the same master weaver[13]. Like their masters, they too specialised in the types of silk they made. The "late ingenious Mr. Lemon", who was both a manufacturer and a pattern drawer, is the only man known to have been thus qualified. Only John Vansommer among the designers belonged to a partnership, Ogier, Vansommer and Triquet of Spital Square; most of the other designers worked freelance, by contrast with the Lyon industry.

Both thrown and raw silk was imported by general merchants who handled many other goods as well from Italy, from China by the East India Company and from Persia via Turkey by the Levant Company. Different qualities were needed for warp and weft and for different kinds of woven material and these came from different places. Bengal silk was being imported by the mid 18th century, but its quality was always low and extremely variable – right up to the 1820s[14]. Brokers found suitable customers for the overseas merchants. The supply of raw silk was always a problem for the English industry (in southern France the French grew some of the best silk they needed and were also nearer to Piedmont from where some of the most useful silk came). Unsuccessful attempts were made to bring silk to England through Russia, to cut out the Turkish middle man, and other attempts were made to grow it in the American Colonies. The Southern Colonies had a suitable climate but not a suitable skilled labour force; slaves could not be expected to tend silk worms with the loving care they needed and this attempt also failed. Silk was thrown (the equivalent of spinning in other industries) in London, but also quite soon outside. Sir Thomas Lombe set up an organzine mill in Derby on the river Derwent on the Italian model, for the making of the thread which was essential for the warp of the fabric, and after his patent expired other Midland towns set up silk works.

By the middle of the century Macclesfield, Congleton and

Leek had important silk mills for which a good water supply and plenty of cheap female and child labour were needed. It was not as unhealthy a trade as cotton spinning and a writer of a letter to a newspaper in 1765 was able to explain with pride that children from three years old could be employed[15]. Only boys could be apprenticed as silk weavers and control over entry was kept quite firmly throughout this period by the Weavers Company – which was greatly strengthened by a money-making exercise of 1740 aimed at recruiting all the Huguenot masters on to its livery. The inscriptions on the designs of James Leman show the structure of the industry. An independent master – James Leman, or his father Peter Leman in earlier years – received a commission from a mercer, so Leman puts on his design "This pattern for an orrace tissue brocaded with gold and silk. For Mr. Wittington [the mercer] & Comp...for my father Peter Leman, by me James Leman, to be made by young Philip Manekey"[16]. When Joseph Dandridge was working for Leman he evidently submitted his design to Leman, who approved it, and Dandridge then provided the draft, the essential stage between the design and the loom. On plate 11 he has written "Mr. Dandridge to finish this as soon as he may" and since the *design* is finished we can deduce that Dandridge then made the draft, incorporating any changes Leman might have wanted. This was normal practice also later in the century[17].

Situated in London, the centre of fashion, the greatest port in the country, the seat of government, finance, insurance and the legislature, the English silk industry had very great advantages denied to Lyon, several hundred miles from Paris, even more from the nearest port, and beset by internal customs barriers. By 1699 the English industry had won the exclusion of Persian and Indian woven silks and these Acts were strengthened later. A long campaign from 1719 to 1721 secured the prohibition of the use and wear of printed calicoes and, even more important, in 1722 a drawback of the duty on silks when they were exported[18]. The expanding North American market made this a most relevant measure[19]. The "Manchester" Act of 1736 permitted the printing of British made fustians with a linen warp and a cotton weft and the calico printers survived. Some types of half-silk (silk and wool or silk and linen) were possibly superseded by cotton. Otherwise, in the first half of the 18th century, the worst problems were created by the periodic shortages of raw silk, partly overcome by temporary legislation. The import of French silks which might – or might not – have paid a high duty was of continuing concern[20]. Proximity to the Commissioners for Trades and Plantations and to Parliament itself meant that the industry, through its representatives on the Court of the Weavers Company, was able to fight off the last attempts at sumptuary legislation in 1743 – and they kept a very watchful eye upon all measures going through Parliament which affected any of the textile trades.

The industry achieved commercial success for a number of reasons. It met the demands of fashion at home. Its quality and dyestuffs were excellent. The English commercial organisation of banks, insurance companies, reliable carriers, good ships properly built and provisioned, supported by factories in foreign ports in Portugal, Danzig, Leghorn, etc., was essential to this industry for all its raw materials were imported. The export trade was protected by the Navigation Acts and British command of the sea. The general economic switch of trade from the Mediterranean to the North Atlantic benefitted the English silk industry, for it brought with it large numbers of piecemeal orders. Even if silks never amounted to more than 1-2% of English overseas trade, this represented prosperity and expansion for one small district of London and an extensive production of textiles which are works of art in their own right.

SILK WEAVING TECHNIQUES

Flowered silks were woven on a drawloom, a combination of wood and string which could be knocked up by any carpenter in Spitalfields. Few specialist loom makers were settled in the district, only reed makers because this part of the loom which spread the warp had to be accurate. The drawloom gave individual control of the warp threads but, because of the problems of friction, control was in groups of from 3 to 10 threads rather than singly as the later jacquard mechanism was able to achieve. This gives the characteristically stepped outline of a drawloom woven silk. The designer had to understand the loom and what it could do. As the article on silk designing in the *Laboratory or School of Arts,* 1756 edition, explained, he must "save the waste of silver on the wrong side of the silk;

and on the other hand to keep the number of shuttles or the workmanship as low as possibly he can, except it be in very rich stuffs, where the price of workmanship is not minded, whether it be two or three shillings per yard more or less"[21]. Leman was careful to make his designs in such a way that the drafts could be done easily and quickly. In the 18th century both silk and metal thread were more expensive than labour, so much use was made of brocading. The warp threads had to be wound on the warp beam or, in the case of a velvet, some on a warp beam and some on individual bobbins and then threaded through the figure harness, the eyes of the heddles on the shafts, and then through the reed and on to the cloth beam. (Understandably, for we are dealing with fine silk threads, apprentices were occasionally "turned over" to other trades because they were "near-sighted"). The cords from the pulley at the top of the figure harness were fixed firmly to the workshop wall and from them hung the cords of the simple. On this, following the draft line by line, a series of *lashes* were tied representing the warp threads which had to be raised for that line. The weaver spent up to three weeks or even longer mounting the loom[22]. To weave he opened the *shed* for the passage of the weft by pressing on a treadle. There might be several wefts in one pass, firstly the weft forming the ground and then pattern wefts going across the loom or brocaded wefts. For each of these his drawboy or drawgirl pulled the lash at the side of the loom. There could be several thousand lashes for a long and multi-coloured pattern. Progress was therefore slow – a yard or two a day was good. The journeyman had to keep his drawboy and the quill winders who got ready the bobbins for the shuttles of the weft. If a sack-back dress took about 14 yards it would take him about a week and a half to make. The more complicated silks were very expensive and normally only four pieces were made to a pattern[23]. Leman saved time by keeping looms ready for different kinds of silk. He says a pattern is to be made, for instance, "in the satin tissue harness". Damasks, looked upon as "common things", were rather quicker to make since there was only one weft for each line of the design.

One small sample of the draft can be seen in plate 107. The numbers at the bottom of the designs enable the draft to be made on "rule paper" or "point paper". The larger numbers like "400" are the numbers of individual cords on which the design repeats, dezines are the length and "8 & 10" the proportion: 8 small divisions horizontally and 10 vertically within each dezine. Since all the colours and different effects had to be written out separately, unless they could be painted on one line as in Leman's instruction on plate 17, the draft would be longer than the pattern.

Certain types of design imposed certain technical rules and certain aesthetic limitations. The designs illustrated here are for tissues, damasks, brocades, tobines, one grogram, velvets, satin and several different kinds of tabby, double tabby, paduasoy, taffeta and lustring. Many effects could be combined. Brocaded details could be introduced into tobines; damask grounds could receive a brocaded polychrome pattern (plate 78); flush patterns could be added, in which an extra self-coloured weft floats in the ground of the fabric. Tobines and flush effects would give contrasting effects according to the way the light reflected from the silk. Different kinds of metal thread gave perhaps the richest texture (plates 69, 70 for example) – not easy to photograph, but easy to visualise its sumptuous effect in a candlelit ballroom. Gold and silver strip (genuine precious metals and not alloys) were used. Gold was made by gilding silver strip. This could be used as a flat strip, "plate", wound on a silk core, "plain", or with one end twisted as in a crepe thread, "frost"; the latter should be used sparingly according to Joubert de l'Hiberderie's essay on the subject[24]. Throughout the century metal threads were drawn to a colour code which should be borne in mind when looking at the designs. Usually shades of yellow, orange and red are used to represent the different kinds, although occasionally another colour is used and on several designs there is a key.

SILKS AND SILK DESIGNS, LATE 17TH CENTURY TO 1730

Although the development of silk design can be followed from the 1670s, by which time there was a sizeable English silk industry, the lack of documented English pieces makes commentary impossible. The loss of the pattern book in the Brussels fire is irretrievable. Plate 1 is possibly an English silk. Although its original provenance is slightly garbled, it had royal associations and was reputed to be English. It could have been supplied to Charles II and date from 1670 when such decorated stripes were fashionable. A very similar silk is worn by Prince Maffeo Barberini in his bust dating from 1670[25]. These formal stripes swiftly gave way to the proto-bizarre[26] designs of the 1680s and 90s, a style which was compounded of exotic elements taken from artifacts imported from India, the East Indies, and China, indiscriminately combined with the current European taste for bulbous Baroque scrolls. The fully fledged "bizarre" silks of about 1700-05[27] contain some of the most extraordinary shapes to be introduced into silk design before the brief and equally extreme phase of *art nouveau* in the early 20th century. Both, curiously, share certain features: the designs are elongated with a marked diagonal slant, a great sense of movement, and plant forms pulled out and distorted until their resemblance to a living plant is hard to discern. This extreme phase was past when James Leman's first surviving designs begin in 1706. The designs, acquired by the museum in 1991, enable some silks to be attributed to Spitalfields with confidence. Leman worked for his father until the latter's death in 1713 and at least one of his early designs is "taken from one of Mr. Budwines"[28] so that we can deduce that Christopher Baudouin "the first that brought the flower'd silk manufacture in credit and reputation here in England"[29] worked for Peter Leman before his son James was old enough to do so. In the later phases of the bizarre style, from 1706 to 1712, the more extreme forms were first replaced with plants of disproportionate size juxtaposed in various ways, then from 1707 to 1708 by designs in which archways, pergolas, canopies and diagonal fences and panels play an important part and which include all manner of quite recognisable and disparate objects; "...pitchforks, and hangers, ropes and ladders, seashells upon trees...have been...thought proper devices for a lady's dress"[30] and this writer recalled a very successful design which sold well made from "sprats upon a gridiron" which were transformed into a silver brocade lutestring. The silk on plate 4 is a good example. The Englishness of this style lies on the one hand in the precipitate retreat from the most extreme bizarre style and on the other in the attempt to give an orderly, balanced structure to design. Wherever possible the odd shapes are not totally abstract but quite recognisably sprats upon a gridiron or whatever. In the next two years the scale was reduced and there were many designs with marked elements of *chinoiserie* and *japonaiserie;* there is even a silk in a private collection with a mock Gujarati inscription woven in the border. Imaginary elements are combined with motifs from Japanese lacquer and other objects on plate 3. This may be compared with a design by James Leman dating from 1709[31] and the portrait of Isaac de Peyster, a New York merchant of Dutch extraction, whose brother Johannes travelled to England and to Rotterdam in 1707-08. De Peyster's silk could have come as an order from London or Rotterdam or could have been bought for him by Johannes.

In the early years of the next decade the amorphous bizarre shapes retreat into the background, while the foreground is occupied by increasingly profuse semi-naturalistic flowers. These are presented quite flatly and often outlined in another colour: pink outlined with red, pale blue outlined with a darker blue, for example. These are lively, cheerful patterns (plates 5, 6), the brocaded sprig on plate 5 deriving from a European view of Persian flowers. Plate 12 by James Leman is typical. It can be compared with the waistcoat worn by Joseph Collet in his portrait figure by Amoy Chinqua, made in 1716, and now in the National Portrait Gallery. The progress of silk design in the middle and later 'teens can be followed both in the Leman designs and in a series of official portraits[32]. The designs which are by James Leman himself tend to be for the lighter materials, lustrings, etc., while Joseph Dandridge seems to have designed the heavier and more elaborate ones for him. Joubert[33] commented upon the fact that French designers tended to specialise in those materials they did best and it is interesting to find English ones doing the same, especially so since there is a splendid English contradiction here. Whereas James Leman had a small collection of natural history specimens, Joseph Dandridge was one of the noted naturalists of his day, a friend of many famous scientists and owner of a large collection reflecting his interests as an ornithologist, entomologist and botanist[34]. Dandridge was a man who went on botanical excursions to Highgate Woods with his distinguished friends when he could get away from his "business", the designing of silks. He even wrote two treatises, one on spiders and one on caterpillars. The contradiction between hobby and work when apparently so closely related is perhaps a thoroughly English idiosyncracy, for it is the least naturalistic designs which are by Dandridge. Compare the designs by Dandridge, plates 31, 32, for example, with those by Leman, plates 33, 34. Plate 8 is one of the few Dandridge

designs in a lighter style. It may be compared with the child by Watteau illustrated by Thornton[35]. The years from 1718 to 1722 were one of the many periods when stripes were in fashion in the 18th century, either broad as in plates 8 and 9 by Leman, or narrow and decorated, as in plates 13 and 33. Asymmetrical designs were very important in the late 'teens. If plate 14 is compared with plate 15 two tendencies can be discerned: firstly a greater refinement in execution and secondly the use of diapered panels of decoration. This design is asymmetrical, but if very slightly rearranged to be a point repeat, like the adjacent design, plate 16, we have the beginnings of the "lace" patterns which lasted until 1731-32. The serpentine decoration of plate 16 and the central group would occur in many subsequent patterns. Plate 17 is a much lighter version and there is at least one waistcoat very similar to this design[36]. The asymmetrical designs with luxuriant vegetation and scrolls in gold and silver between them covering nearly all the ground are the ones most often seen in official portraits, for these were the most expensive silks, suitable for kings and plenipotentiaries; plate 19 is an example. The silver lustring was a much more popular choice for social occasions and Leman designed many of them. The silk on plate 20 may be compared with Leman's designs on plates 35 and 28 and many other silks (e.g., T.88B-1978). At a wedding attended by Mrs. Pendarves in 1724 "Mrs. Rolle was in a pink and silver lutestring and Mrs. Walpole in a white gold and silver but not so pretty as Mrs. Rolle's"[37] and various others are noted by her on other occasions.

The transformation of the asymmetrical patterns of the late 'teens into the lace patterns of the twenties can be seen by looking at two Dandridge designs of 1720, plates 30, 29. Their choice of motif is very similar, but 30 has a straight repeat, while 29 has a point repeat and under the brocaded metal thread a diapered damask pattern. Although the first art historian to describe these patterns as "lace" was Otto von Falke, their similarity to lace was already noticed by Mrs. Delany in 1729, when she described a dress she wore as having "a running pattern like lace in the ground"[38]. What she failed to realise and my colleague Miss Levey has shown[39] is that the silk patterns influenced the lace and not vice versa. The designer Anna Maria Garthwaite possessed an important group of "Patterns by different Hands" dating from the mid 1720s, before she herself came to London to live with her twice-widowed sister, Mary Danny, in the heart of Spitalfields. These designs include the four on plates 39-42, dating from 1724 to 1726. All are by Christopher Baudouin, the most famous designer of his day, who had, as we have seen, worked for the Lemans. He was associated with the Lekeux family, one of the most important families of master weavers in the industry, was a loyal member of the Vestry of what became Christ Church, Spitalfields, and signed the Petition for 50 New Churches as one of the Principal Inhabitants[40]. His designs, good or bad, are a key to the standard English production expected to reach and it was probably a deliberate choice by Garthwaite to acquire his work rather than that of any other designer of the time. His touch is lighter than that of Leman and thus it is likely that plate 38 is Leman's work, for it is much less delicate. All five patterns lie midway between the exotic fruit backed by the damask forms harking back to the "bizarre" and the more pronounced plant forms of the later twenties. At this point lace and floral motifs are evenly balanced and, on the whole, the grounds are open so that the ground weave plays an important part in the decoration. Unfortunately, no silks by Leman, Dandridge or Christopher Baudouin have so far come to light[41] but their designs enable the silks on plates 22, 23 to be attributed to Spitalfields and to this date. Plate 23 may be compared especially with plate 40. The fresh colouring in both cases is typically English. It is as if they were painted in daylight as opposed to the muted – or subtler? – tones of French silks. The colouring of English silks is a characteristic which, once noted, is easily distinguished. While plate 22 is in Leman's style, plate 23 has some of the nervous grace of Baudouin's designs. The dating of plate 21 to 1726-28 rests upon a comparison, on the one hand with plate 43, dated 1728, and on the other with French designs of the period. The majority of English silks were half ell wide, but in fact about 19-21 inches or less[42] while the French half ell wide are rather wider, 22-23 inches. Plate 24 is a typical lace pattern and can be compared with plate 38 which is probably by James Leman, with the French designs in the Bibliothèque Nationale, and with three paintings by Mercier of the daughters of George II[43]. Plate 25 shows the richest and most elaborate kind of lace pattern in which the ground of the fabric has virtually disappeared beneath the gold thread. The silk is framed with

silver tabby and lined with white taffeta. According to family tradition it formed part of the canopy used at George II's Coronation in 1727 and this tradition is supported by other evidence. The construction is the same as that said to have been used at the Coronation of George I. The style of the silks is correct for their date in both cases, and accords with the brief description in the Royal Accounts[44]. The earlier silk was, however, supplied by Anthony Levany, merchant, and was thus imported, while this silk was supplied by George Binckes, a mercer of Bedford Street, Covent Garden, a retailer. He had supplied silks to the Crown over a long period but he had also commissioned designs from James Leman. It is even possible from its style that this silk was designed by Leman (since he had a considerable reputation), but no designs of his survive from this date[45]. The epitome of the lace pattern is represented by plate 26. This silk exploits the varying textures of silk and silver thread to the full. It was surely a material like this which Mrs. Delany was wearing when she described her clothes in 1729 – although she said that hers was French. Very little plain ground is left, but there is a balance between the floral and the decorative elements. Without the survival of Baudouin's designs it would be presumptuous to ascribe such a material to Spitalfields. The last two designs in this group are by Garthwaite. They date from 1728 and 1729, respectively, and were probably executed in London, but they show her debt to the Baudouin designs which she possessed. The colour scheme of plate 43 suggests that it was probably intended for metal thread, while plate 44 was probably for metal thread and coloured silks or, alternatively, for a silk with a brocaded pattern on a damask ground.

As well as the consistent evolution of the lace patterns – the heavier versions woven as tissues and the lighter as lustrings – there are other designs which defy any neat aesthetic classification. Garthwaite's earliest designs "1726 in York – Before I came to London" include patterns which do not always seem to be for silks[46]. Among these is the design on plate 27. This has a straight repeat but has no parallel among existing woven silks. Books of "Chinese" patterns were, however, beginning to appear, as far removed from the real thing as the japonaiserie in plate 3.

Between 1730 and 1732 a complete revolution in design took place, a revolution completed by 1735. The lace patterns of the 1720s had exploited to the full the possible textures of a flat woven design in a way which is difficult to appreciate without seeing them without glass. They reflect the light differently from the different weaves – satin, twill or tabby and from the differing textures of silks and metal thread. Now fashion demanded not texture, but an illusion of three dimensional form. Already, the floral elements had begun to break through the lace framework of the last of the lace patterns. The latter retreated until it reached the vestigial form of plate 45. The narrow curves at the sides of this silk would be difficult to understand without a knowledge of the lace patterns which had come before. In Garthwaite's designs the ultimate stage was reached when even this outline vanishes and only the formal arrangement of the flowering motifs show where it has been, plates 57-61. Plate 58 has the typical diapered panels; in plate 57 the floral elements are very pronounced and even more so in plate 60; plate 61, dated 1732, has very large floral motifs and plate 59, a "gold stuff" also from 1732, no lace, only the elaborate central motif. Whereas the stately and formal lace pattern was invariably designed with a point repeat, such an arrangement was a constraint upon the new style and from 1732 until about 1749 straight repeats are nearly always found.

The dress of which a detail is shown on plate 48 is one of the last of the formally composed designs. It has a point repeat but no lace and may be compared with a dress worn by the Princess Royal when she married William, Prince of Orange, in March 1734. The descriptions of the silks worn at this wedding may be compared with those worn at her brother's wedding two years later. In March 1734 "the newest fashioned silks were white paduasoys with large flowers of tulips, peonies, emmonies (sic), carnations & etc. in their proper colours, some wove in the silk and some embroidered"[47]. The King wore to his son's wedding "a gold brocade turn'd with silk, embroider'd with large Flowers in silver and colours" and the "waistcoats were universally brocades, with large flowers"[48]. But while Ann herself had had two sumptuous materials sent over from France, it was observed at her brother's wedding that "most of the rich clothes were the Manufacture of England",

and the *Gentleman's Magazine* considered that the French silks which were worn were much inferior to the British! One thing is certain: the silks worn at the two weddings could be distinguished from one another and it is interesting that, rightly or wrongly, the *Gentleman's Magazine* thought that it could recognise which were English – and preferred them.

The earliest silk which has come to light which can be precisely dated by a Garthwaite design is plate 47, dating from 1733. Its narrow width – $15^1/_2$ inches – and slightly odd colouring present complications. It could have been woven by Daniel (?) Booth from the design illustrated. He could also have woven it with the alterations he thought necessary to make it acceptable to the Dutch market – just as the French put on the seals of Brabant to make their silks acceptable to markets otherwise closed to French silks. On the other hand, it could have been a Dutch silk from which Garthwaite took her design, hence the slight differences between the design itself and the silk, or even a copy by the Dutch of the silk designed by Garthwaite and hence the differences in design[49]. One of James Leman's early designs was "taken from a Dutch stuff" in 1711 and one or two others he had taken from French silks.

The initiative for rendering three dimensional effects in silk design came from Lyon. In England "about the year 1732 three designers attempted to introduce the principles of painting into the loom and succeeded. Mr. John Vansommer (... instructed in the principles...of drawing for the loom by Mr. Dandridge...), Mrs. Anna Maria Garthwaite, and Mr. Peter Mazell"[50]. This is one of the points at which it is possible to isolate and to recognise a certain "Englishness". The first to try to render such effects was a Lyon designer named Courtois, who did so by laying tones of colour side by side, using much black for dramatic effect. His favourite motif seems to have been a large tree of pre-historic appearance, on a tiny island in space, from which hang flowers and fruit of a disproportionate size. This was much too strong meat for the English palate[51] but, when Anglicised, the motif of a tree upon an island became extremely popular. Instead of a motif from a feverish nightmare we have a stylised version of an English woodland tree, often with a cottage or a castle at its foot. Plates 49 and 50 may be compared with plates 62, 63 by Garthwaite, both dating from 1734. Here, clearly, we have the tendency to prefer the natural and the observed to the fantastical and allegorical.

Garthwaite and her contemporaries in England ignored the theory behind Courtois' work and produced trees. And if it seems extraordinary for fashion in a well-ordered society to decree that large trees should be worn (the repeat of plate 50 is 48 inches long – the life size of a young cherry tree when bought from a nursery!), the portrait of Mrs. Broughton wearing the silk in plate 51 shows that what fashion decreed the customer agreed[52]. The colouring in the silks of this time tends to bright, fresh greens on a white ground. English and also American customers were very partial to silks with a white ground. Whatever discussion there may be about the provenance of the finest lace patterns of a few years earlier, these silks are instantly recognisable as English. We know nothing about the work of Peter Mazell and little about that of John Vansommer, unfortunately, but the "principles of painting" which Garthwaite adopted were those of Jean Revel. As Peter Thornton showed, this talented artist adapted the *points rentrés* of the tapestry weaver which enabled tones of colour to be dovetailed, thus producing a striking sensation of three dimensional form[53]. Garthwaite acquired some of his designs and speedily adapted them. All her designs from 1735 onwards use them. No-one claiming to belong to fashionable society could have gone to Frederick's wedding in 1736 in a dress or a waistcoat which did not have *points rentrés* to shade the flowers.

Since large designs were necessary to show off the possible effects, the scale of design continued to be massive throughout the later thirties. This was the time when designers gave "the size of a cabbage to a rose...and that of a pompkin to an olive;...not many years since [in 1756] the prevailing French fashion among our English ladies"[54]. Plates 64-66 represent these years from 1735-38. In plate 64 the island motif still appears but this had gone by 1736. The *points rentrés* are, however, very clear in plate 64. Plate 52 may be compared with plate 65, the trail of berries being probably a fashionable device of about 1736-37. The enormous scale of plate 54 is even more striking than that of Mrs. Broughton's dress. Plate 55 represents the slightly lighter version of the style and it can be dated by comparison with plate 66, of 1736, and 56, dated 1738. While the branch on the latter looks like a real branch the flowers are basically exotic – its inspiration is again a fanciful view of China. Plate 67 is a more interesting design than first

it seems. Are the curiously diapered panels the remains of the islands of 1734 or versions of the *rocaille* from contemporary grottoes? Is the spiky plant growing from the lower panel an aloe and, if so, what prompted Garthwaite to use this motif and, specifically, to use it in 1738? Although silk design continued to be massive in scale and restricted in colour scheme until 1742 this design gives a preview of Garthwaite's own original contribution to the decorative arts.

Silks and Silk Design, 1740 to 1750

The *Gentleman's Magazine* carried an enthusiastic article in June 1749 on a designer of English silks. "...our incomparable countrywoman by the force of mere natural taste and ingenuity, has made the English loom vie with the Italian pencil, very different from the gaudy patterns of the French, who have never yet with all the Assistance of the Drawing Academy been able to exhibit true proportion or just colouring on silks or linen in any single flower..."[55]. This eulogy could refer to Mrs. Phoebe Wright but we are more inclined to believe that it refers to Garthwaite. It has the same touch of jingoism as Hogarth's remarks about "foreign interlopers" and his conscious wish to turn away from the Grand Manner to what he could observe[56]. Postlethwayt's article compared the "glare of colours" in French silks and their "tawdry tinsel appearances" with English silks which were "pictures of great delicacy and ornament" and the contrast he summed up "as between good sense and affectation". There was a contrary view: Rouquet in his *État des Arts en Angleterre* speaks of "une femme sans art et sans lumière guidée par un caprice ignorant ...depuis longtems la principale source des dessins colorés qu'on y employe"[57] (i.e. in Spitalfields), 1755, p.111. This could also refer to Garthwaite. While there was little change from 1740 to 1742 (plates 68 and 109) the decade from 1742 to 1752 is certainly one in which English silk design owed very little to French. If there is a recognisable English style it is most discernible then. Whether it merited the eulogies of Postlethwayt or the abhorrence of Rouquet's article must be determined by looking at the plates. One thing is indisputable. The English and the French seem to have approached their task with very different aims.

The years from 1740 to 1742 are transitional in style just as those from 1730 to 1732 had been. Plate 100 is a lightweight silk but its date in August 1740 meant that it was intended for a winter season. The gnarled root is perhaps a development of the panel we saw in 1738. Its floral style is entirely non-naturalistic, but the scale is subtly lighter and much of the intrinsic quality of the silk is revealed. The design when woven becomes an acceptable and attractive silk with a much subtler repeat than appears from the design (plate 99). Garthwaite's designs also show some of the other varieties of silk: plates 102-107 include velvets and a grogram for men's suitings and plate 101 on the same page is a tobine. The most extreme forms of the "large flower" style can be seen in plates 71, 109 and 110. Not only is the design massive in plate 71 but the textured tobine ground makes the material itself heavy. The passion flower in this silk may be one of the motifs popular in a particular year or a particular season, for it appears again in plate 72 . Whereas plate 71 is comparable to Garthwaite's work, the silk facing it is not. There were never many designers for flowered silks in Spitalfields at one time and this must come from one of Garthwaite's rivals. On rather tenuous evidence it is possible that this was Mrs. Wright's. Another ephemeral but remarkable motif seems to be the bursting seed or pea pod, of which plates 79 and 109 are examples.

The year 1742 marks a watershed in Garthwaite's production. From then onwards two books of her designs exist for nearly every year, an average of 80 patterns, and more silks woven from those of 1742 seem to have survived than from any other year. Patterns for damasks continued to be very large and so did those in gold and silver. In "Grand designs for gold and silver stuffs...the gold and silver should always be ornamental, intermixt with mosaick, and at proper places set off with some plate. But the silk brocade must be composed of the smaller sort of natural flowers, coloured and shaded to the greatest perfection"[58]. This description from the *Laboratory* applies well to plate 111, while the silk and the design for it on plates 69, 70 show the highest quality brocaded silver tabbys, as we should expect from Captain Peter Lekeux. Half way through 1742 there was, however, a change in scale. The designs are drawn half size by Garthwaite, while the floral motifs are much closer to real flowers, as in plate 111 from July 1742. By November 1742, in plate 112, the total effect is of flowers of "true proportion" with some recognisable varieties such as the bladder campion at the top right hand side.

True botanical naturalism arrived in 1743. The designs for this year came to light quite unexpectedly in 1971 and were purchased for the Museum after a public appeal. In these designs and in those for 1744 her work is deliberately based on botanical forms. The indexes which she put in the volumes[59] list "bro[caded] tabby holly leaves" (plate 113), "Aloe leaf" (plate 115) as well as a "tobine lutestring pinks", a "bro. lut[estring] strawberries", a "tobine lut[estring] heartsease". Even when the varieties are not listed in the title the flowers are very clearly delineated in the designs. The aloe leaf seems to have been of considerable interest to her. One example has already been mentioned and the design with aloe leaves is echoed in the silver leaves in the adjacent plate (114). Most of these flowers are commonly found to this day, but there are also more exotic ones delineated with equal care. I am greatly indebted to Miss Margaret Stones for her help in spotting these. Certain flowers emerge as Garthwaite's favourites: auriculas, honeysuckle in 112 and 124, for example, as well as daisies, and the blue convolvulus tricolor.

While Garthwaite takes some artistic licence in combining these plants, their accuracy is sufficiently striking to raise some interesting questions. Fritillaries (plate 113), parrot tulips (plate 118), and daisies (plate 116), she might have seen in any good garden, but where did she see a flower only introduced to this country[60] in 1734, or, indeed, the several varieties of lilies such as those in plate 120, 121? One strong possibility is in the garden of Peter Collinson, a merchant trading to America with his brother James, but also celebrated for his botanical work. Garthwaite's ward, Mary Bacon, was the daughter of an apothecary and naturalist[61] and she herself was a well-educated woman who could have been welcome in such circles. Her style is, however, closest to that of G.D. Ehret who made a deep impression upon botanical circles at the time of his first visit to London in 1735, returning for good in 1737 when the Royal Society purchased a series of his drawings of aloes of several different kinds[62]. Since they did not have a Visitor's Book one can only speculate as to whether Garthwaite saw this series, for it is remarkable that she first used an aloe leaf in 1738. He drew a number of different types of auricula in 1742-43 and, again, Garthwaite uses these flowers throughout the 1740s. Around 1740 there seems to have been one of the periodic revivals of intense interest in botanical studies which were a feature of English life in the 18th century and, possibly, unlike such pursuits in other countries, they were followed by a very wide section of society. Although this can only be a hypothesis (until some personal reference to her turns up, if ever, in the papers of a botanist of the time) it seems likely that she both visited celebrated gardens in which newly imported plants were growing and in their delineation was profoundly influenced by Ehret's work – whether she saw his drawings in someone's house or met and talked to the man himself. The exhibition of *Flowers in Art* held at the British Museum in the spring of 1979 made it possible to compare the published treatises of the period with her designs and none has much affinity either in choice of subject or in style with Garthwaite's work.

Between 1743 and 1745 Anna Maria Garthwaite drew some 206 patterns and sold 205, containing a profusion of realistically rendered flowers. Only a few can be illustrated. Plate 75 and 76 are a design from 1744 and the silk woven from it, with her favourite auriculas and convolvulus. In plates 77, 78, an elaborate silk of the highest quality, there are a number of different flowers including blue larkspur and a Turk's Cap or similar lily. The silks of these years are some of the highest achievements of the English silk industry and are probably the best of Garthwaite's own production. Among the lighter range of silks are two with what looks like string, plates 73, 74, which can be dated by comparison with a Garthwaite design of 1743[63]. This consists only of lightly tied bunches of pink and white string, presumably another of the ephemeral motifs already seen in other years.

The study of botanical detail was perfectly compatible with the aesthetic styles of the time. The Line of Beauty has been discussed earlier. The asymmetrical cartouches which are one of the essential features of the Rococo can be seen in the ground pattern of the silk plate 85 and in plate 120, as well as many other Garthwaite designs not illustrated here. *Rocaille,* which gave its name to the style – a kind of stylised rock formation from the fashionable grottoes of the time – was drawn by Garthwaite in a design of 1745 (plate 82) and its effect can be seen in a very similar silk on the same plate. Another version, half rock, half root, appears in a design of 1747, plate 125. A little outside her normal repertoire is the "Bro. tabby India", plate 117, for which a Chinese painted silk must have been the model, a reminder that chinoiseries could

be adapted to the style of every period. She drew another version in the same year for a different weaver. Like the chinoiserie earlier in the century the plant is not much like real bamboo but an excuse for the exotic, in contradiction to most of her work at the time (a perversity which could be considered another English trait?). Interestingly, American importers also made no distinction between Indian and Chinese silks, all of which were handled by the East India Company anyway.

The designs for 1746 are still missing and we can only attribute silks to this year by comparison with the designs for 1745 and 1747. Plate 83, for example, is a fairly rare striped silk of the time, with some of Garthwaite's favourite flowers, auriculas, carnations and rosebuds.

Giving evidence to the House of Commons many years later John Sabatier said that the most prosperous years he could remember were from 1748 to 1750[64] so it is interesting to see what the silks from then looked like. Two changes can be noticed from 1747 to 1749: there is a narrower choice of flowers (nearly every design or silk has carnations or roses rather than the botanical diversity of the earlier 1740s) and, secondly, the grounds of the fabrics were becoming increasingly elaborate. Casually strewn sprays of flowers seem more common than the densely packed designs seen so far. Very typical are plates 86, 87, with brocaded flowers on an elaborate tobine ground, and 90, 91, with a brocaded spray on a pale coffee coloured ground, a fashionable colour of the time. (This is the "sad" colour so often requested by American merchants in their correspondence with England). Sometimes the flowers are loosely tied in a bunch as in plate 126, dating from 1747, and the silk in plate 80, in which the ribbon is made by the ground pattern as it is also in plate 96. The design and silk in plates 92, 93, dating from 1748, is the only case apart from the silk of 1733 in which the silk and its design have any important differences. Thomas Brant has changed the colour of the branch, the weight of the material, and has added a slightly fussy self-coloured pattern in tune with the demand for figured grounds but, no doubt, annoying to Garthwaite. "Some weavers, to show their own taste and judgement, will frequently cause a pattern drawer to alter a good design...and by that means murder the design, and make it deformed, without any coherence, taste, or humour; with which the pattern drawer is obliged to comply, if he values his custom"[65].

Garthwaite's greatest rival at this time was probably John Vansommer whose work we can now only identify by his reputation and by one silk which has passed down to his descendants. On this basis, plate 89 can be tentatively attributed to him. The ribbons in the design suggest an earlier date and the basket appears in a Garthwaite design of 1745, but a similar one is carried by Lucy Ebberton in her portrait by Knapton in Dulwich College Picture Gallery so this was probably a popular accessory for several years. The silk facing this, plate 88, is surely by yet another designer. Two other silks by unknown designers must be considered; plate 95 has a rare point repeat and a strange pattern in the ground, whose elaboration suggests the end of the 1740s, and plate 94, with musical trophies and Union Jacks. Such a patriotic silk ought to be easily traced. Handel's Te Deum to celebrate the victory of Dettingen (when, for the last time, an English king led his troops into battle) was first performed on November 27th, 1743. However, during the summer of 1745, after the invasion of the Young Pretender, a new anthem was being sung in the theatres by a standing audience to great applause. It began "God save our gracious King...". In the autumn of 1746, after the defeat of the Young Pretender, another anthem was composed. Whereas the fashion correspondents of the newspapers industriously noted the silks worn at royal weddings, no-one apparently noticed this silk. Perhaps it may be found among the missing Garthwaite designs for 1746, for the style could be hers.

An emphasis on patterned grounds, on "ornaments with mosaick", dominated 1749. Plate 127 and 128 are characteristic and the deceptively simple design in plate 130 was probably intended for a watered flowered tabby. There is just such a silk in the Museum of the City of New York and a young member of an expatriate Jacobite family wears one in her portrait by Vishnyakov in the Russian Museum in Leningrad [66]. These materials continued in fashion into the early 1750s. Mrs. Delany described the dress of a lady of her acquaintance as "white and silver, mosaic ground, flowered with silver intermixed with a little blue"[67].

Much of the historic evidence about the silk industry comes from the 1765 and 1766 reports to the Select Committee of the House of Commons which investigated the silk trade. It refers back over a long period and one remark made by a pattern drawer, Peter Cheveney, makes a fitting conclusion. He told the Committee "that the working after our own invention gives a different taste from the French and a fairer chance of the Export Trade than copying from French designs, because Foreigners will not choose to take from you at second hand what they can get from the French at first ..."[68]. Thus it is that the silks of this decade, when the English did follow their own inventions, can be found in every country with which England had close trading links: Scandinavia (excluding Sweden), Ireland, Scotland, Holland and, above all, the American Colonies whose increasing wealth made them important consumers of luxury goods.

NOTES

1. Sir Nicholas Pevsner, *The Englishness of English Art*, London, 1955, p.19.
2. F. Breghot du Lut (editor), *Le Livre de Raison de Jacques Charles Dutillieu*, Lyon, 1769, published 1886, p.47.
3. Rouquet, *L'Etat des Arts en Angleterre*, 1755, pp.110-111, 114.
4. Customs 3 Public Record Office. The figures for the exports of woven silks have been abstracted by N. Rothstein, appendix to *The Silk Industry in London 1702-1766*, University of London M. A. Thesis, 1961.
5. Malachy Postlethwayt, *A Dictionary of Trade and Commerce*, 1751, Vol. I, article on *Engraving*.
6. G. Smith, *The Laboratory or School of Arts*, Vol. II, 1756 edition, p.39, para 4. P.Thornton in "An 18th century Silk Designer's Manual", *Bulletin of the Needle and Bobbin Club*, Nos.1 & 2, 1958, pp.7-33, argued very reasonably that Garthwaite was, herself, the author of the article on silk designing, which does not appear in earlier editions.
7. Pevsner, *op. cit.*, p.22.
8. Dept. of Prints and Drawings E.4440-1909 to E.4495-1909 and series 5970-5990, E.1861-1991, Dept. of Textiles T.391 to T.393-1971. Pattern Books T.373-1972, to T.397-

1972. See V&A Museum Departmental Guides, *Textiles and Dress*, London, 1978.
9. P. K. Thornton and N. Rothstein, "The Importance of the Huguenots in the London Silk Industry", *Proceedings of the Huguenot Society of London*, Vol. XX, No.1, p.83; N. Rothstein, "Huguenots in the 18th century English Silk Industry" in I. Scouloudi, *Huguenots in Britain and their French Background 1550-1800*, London, 1987 (there are three editorial mistakes, most importantly there are no Canterbury Quarterage Lists); N. Rothstein "Canterbury and London, the Silk Industry in the late 17th century", *Textile History* vol 20 no.1 Spring 1989 pp.33-47.
10. N. Rothstein, Thesis, pp.13-68.
11. Anon., *A General Description of all Trades*, 1747, p.219.
12. Truman & Hanbury Stock Rest Book, 1767-75, and numerous insurance policies taken out with the Hand in Hand Insurance Company for ale houses.
13. Two pattern books from the Warner Archive, now in the V&A, T.376-1972 and T.379-1972, cover the period 1774-1820. Some of the same journeymen and their families can be traced throughout.
14. House of Commons Papers, 1821 Report on Foreign Trade (Silk and Wine Trade), p.13, evidence of John Thorpe, and p.22, evidence of J.J.E. de Ferre.
15. "Veritas", Gazette and New Daily Advertiser, February 27th 1765.

16. E.1861.45-1991.

17. P.A. de Brissac, *Account Book 1760-1762*, photocopy in the V&A Library. He frequently sold patterns and charged extra for the draft, e.g., "To a model for a flowered satin one colour...£1.10s. To the R.P. [Ruled Paper] of the Above satin 110 cords 12 dez[ines] 8 & 9...6/-June 18 and 19 1762".

18. N. Rothstein, "The Calico Campaign of 1719-21", in *East London Papers*, Vol. VII, No.1, July 1964, pp.3-21.

19. The drawback is mentioned in the many surviving invoices in American merchants' papers. It helped to offset other costs such as insurance and shipping. The subject is discussed in N. Rothstein, "Silks for the American Market", *Connoisseur*, Nov. 1965, p.153.

20. N. Rothstein, Thesis, pp.449-456, and pp.489-504.

21. *Laboratory*, *op. cit.*, p.41.

22. *Gazette and New Daily Advertiser*, March 14th 1765, Letter from "C" in answer to "B"'s queries.

23. *House of Commons Journals*, Report on Silk Manufacture, March 4th 1765, pp.209 and 210, evidence of John Perigal and John Allen .

24. Joubert de L'Hiberderie, *Le dessinateur pour les Etoffes d'or...et de Soie*, Paris, 1774 (first edition 1764), Chapter XIII, p.51.

25. North Mymms Park Sale, Christies, lot 13, Sep. 1979.

26. The description given by Peter Thornton in *Baroque and Rococo Silks*, London, 1965, p.96.

27. Thornton, *op. cit.*, pp.95-102.

28. E.1861. 46-1991

29. *Laboratory*, *op. cit.*, p.43 footnote.

30. *Laboratory*, *op. cit.*, p.43.

31. E. 1861. 102-1991

32. Hyacinthe Rigaud, portrait of Duchess Elizabeth Charlotte of Orleans, 1713, now at Vaux-le-Vicomte; Gobert, Louis XV as dauphin, 1714, in the Prado; Caroline of Ansbach, Princess of Wales, 1716, in the Royal Collection; Enoch Zeeman, Elihu Yale, dated 1717, now at Yale.

33. Joubert, *op. cit.*, Préface, XXIII. The same observation was also made by Paulet in *Le Fabricant des Etoffes de Soie*, Vol. VII, part 2, p.885 [Paris, Académie des Sciences. Descriptions des Arts et Métiers, Tome IX.]

34. D.E. Allen, "Joseph Dandridge and the first Aurelian Society", *Entomologists Record*, 78, 89-94; W.S. Bristowe "The Life and Work of a Great English Naturalist Joseph Dandridge 1664-1746", *Entomologists Gazette*, Vol. 18, pp.73-89 and "More about Joseph Dandridge and his friends James Petiver and Eleazar Albin", pp.197-211; N. Rothstein, "Joseph Dandridge Naturalist and Silk Designer" in *East London Papers*, Vol.9, No.2, Winter 1966, pp.101-118.

35. Thornton, *op. cit.*, pl. 52b.

36. The Royal Albert Memorial Museum, Exeter, 7/1965/3.

37. *Autobiography and Correspondence of Mary Granville, Mrs. Delany*, edited by Lady Llanover, 3 Vols., 1861, Vol.I, p.96.

38. Mrs. Delany, *op. cit.*, p. 198.

39. S. Levey, "Lace and lace-patterned silks: some comparative illustrations", in *Studies in Textile History*, edited by V. Gervers, Royal Ontario Museum, 1977, pp.184-202.

40. Lambeth Palace Library, Papers of the Commissioners for 50 New Churches.

41. One silk, after Leman's design E.1861.80-1991 of 1710, has been identified in Adelaide, Art Gallery of New South Wales.

42. N. Rothstein, Thesis, pp.251-252.

43. Cabinet des Estampes, Vol. Lh 44a. The Mercier paintings belong to Hertford Borough Council.

44. 1714 L.C. 2 (20) i., 1727 L.C. 2. 21.

45. Although no designs later than 1722 have survived, James Leman was in active partnership with Jacob Leman, possibly his brother in 1732. See N. Rothstein, "The successful and the unsuccessful Huguenot, another look at the London silk industry" in *Proceedings of the Huguenot Society* vol. XXV, no.5 1993, p.443.

46. Some are similar in style to a paper-cut acquired in 1993 by the V&A, signed Anna Maria Garthwaite and dated 1707 (E.1077-1993).

47. *London Evening Post*, March 14th-16th 1734.

48. *Gentleman's Magazine*, Vol. VI, April 1736, p.231.

49. Evidence for an 18th century silk industry in Holland is set out in N. Rothstein, "Dutch Silks – An important but forgotten industry of the 18th century or a hypothesis?" *Oud Holland*, No. 3, Jg. LXXIX, 1964, pp.152-172.

50. Postlethwayt, *op. cit.*

51. An example is illustrated by Thornton, plate 63a.

52. Illustrated in N. Rothstein, *Silk Designs of the Eighteenth Century in the Collection of the Victoria and Albert Museum*, 1990.

53. P.K. Thornton, "Jean Revel, Dessinateur de la Grande Fabrique", *Gazette des Beaux-Arts*, July 1960, pp.71-86.

54. *Laboratory*, p.39.

55. *Gentleman's Magazine*, June 1749, Vol. XIX, p.319.

56. Discussed by Pevsner, *op. cit.*, pp.20-22.

57. Rouquet, *op. cit.*

58. *Laboratory*, p.41.

59. The designs for each year are divided into two volumes and indexed under the names of the weavers who bought them. All the designs were published in N.Rothstein, *Silk Designs of the Eighteenth Century in the Collection of the Victoria and Albert Museum*, 1990.

60. T.392-1971, p.3, pink Kalmia Latifolia. I am much indebted to Miss Stones for giving up her time to examine the Garthwaite designs for their botanical content.

61. Vincent Bacon; see D.E. Allen, "John Martyn's Botanical Society: A Biographical Analysis of the Membership", *Proceedings of the Botanical Society of the British Isles*, Vol. 6, pt. 4, May 1967, p.310.

62. Royal Society, Drawings of Plants bought by the Society in 1737 [LXXII d. 14].

63. T.391-1971, p.67.

64. House of Commons Journals, April 14th 1766, Silk Manufacture Evidence to Select Committee, p.725.

65. *Laboratory*, p.40.

66. Museum of the City of New York, 60. 9. 1b, dress of Hannah Allen, reputed to date from 1763, but surely 1753? Portrait of Sarah Fermor, later Countess Yakov, by I.Y. Vishnyakov (1699-1761), painted in 1750 when she was ten years old. 5989.26, dated 1752, by Anna Maria Garthwaite, shows a similar design, of which there is a silk T.10-1962.

67. Mrs. Delany, *op. cit.*, III, p.300.

68. 1765 report, pp.211-212.

WORSTEDS

Fine quality worsteds for costume and furnishings were made in London and East Anglia from the 15th century onwards as well as other places in Northern France and the Low Countries. The wool for such materials was combed as well as carded, to give a smooth surface in the woven material. Sheep were bred with a slightly different and less curly fleece to provide suitable wool. The earliest surviving samples of English worsteds date from 1719 and there are other samples in Paris and Stockholm dating from the middle of the 18th century[1]. Plain and striped worsteds were used both as linings and as materials in their own right. Worsted damasks were important, both as bed furnishings and for men's waistcoats and banyans, but far fewer survive than their equivalents in silk. Although tough and hard-wearing, any woollen material is subject to attack by moth.

Worsteds made with drawloom-woven patterns followed the styles of woven silks, though their colours were often brighter and many were glazed. Plate 7 can be dated by comparison with silks to the early 18th century, for such stripes with fine floral patterns can be found in late 17th century materials. Significantly, it was found in Portugal, to which there was a very large export trade in English worsteds – though even more went to the American Colonies. In the first half of the 18th century both Spitalfields and Norwich made these materials, which were advertised on the trade cards of the same mercers who sold the finest silks. Gradually Norwich came to dominate production, though "town made camlets" and similar descriptions continued to be advertised until the 1770s at least. Originally a glazed striped material, "calimanco" became a generic term for all fine worsteds. Of the two later examples, plate 98 probably dates from the middle of the century, while plate 97 is difficult to date closely. It is possible that patterns continued to be current longer than in silks. This may have depended on the market, for there are many requests by American merchants writing to England for "fashionable" worsteds and complaints when those shipped were not – when, for example, small flowers were sent when large flowers were in fashion.

NOTES

1. Public Record Office, C.O. 388. 21, No. 209, fols, 146-153; Paris, Musée des Arts Décoratifs, "Livres d'Echantillons contenant les diverses Etoffes qui se farbiquent dans l'Etendue de la province de Lankashire en Angleterre...présenté à M. de Montigny...", c.1750, gathered by John Holker; in Stockholm the collection of Anders Berch contains four pattern books of Norwich worsteds. See *18th Century Textiles: The Anders Berch Collection at the Nordiska Museet*, ed. E. Hidemark, Stockholm, 1990.

PLATES

1. Woven silk. Third quarter 17th century.
Repeat, 7 x 8½ in. (18 x 21.5 cm)
This silk is thought to have been used by Charles II.
T.14-1922.

2. Striped worsted damask. Norwich or Spitalfields,
about 1720-30.
26 x 12 in. (66 x 30.5 cm)
T.675-1974.

3. *Japonaiserie,* woven silk. Spitalfields or Holland, about 1709.
Repeat, 19¾ x 9¹³/₁₆ in. (50.2 x 25 cm) Two repeats in width
of fabric.
T.173-1965.

4. Woven silk. Spitalfields, about 1707-08.
Damask brocaded in coloured silks.
32 x 20¼ in. (81.5 x 51.5 cm)
711-1864.

5. Christening blanket. Spitalfields or Holland, about 1711-12.
Silk damask brocaded in colours.
Repeat, 13½ x 8¾ in. (34 x 22 cm)
T.225-1973.

6. Woven silk. Spitalfields, about 1712-15.
Damask brocaded in coloured silks.
Repeat, 21½ x 8½ in. (55 x 22 cm)
T.148A-1968.

7. Chasuble, detail of material. Norwich or Spitalfields,
early 18th century.
Striped worsted.
Repeat, 8 x 6¾ in (20 x 17 cm)
T.287-1962.

8. Silk design by Joseph Dandridge, dated 1718.
Water colour on paper.
18¾ x 10¼ in. (47.5 x 26 cm)
E.4466-1909.

9. Silk design by James Leman, dated 1721.
Water colour on paper.
20½ x 12 in. (52 x 30.5 cm)
E.4450-1909.

10. Silk design by James Leman, dated 1718.
Water colour on paper.
15½ x 10¼ in. (39.5 x 26 cm)
Also inscribed with the name of the mercer, Isaac Tullie, who
commissioned it.
E.4465-1909.

11. Silk design by Joseph Dandridge for James Leman,
dated 1719.
Water colour on paper.
16½ x 10¾ in. (42 x 27 cm)
Also inscribed with the name of the mercer, Isaac Tullie,
who commissioned it.
E.4471-1909.

12. Silk design by James Leman, about 1717.
Water colour on paper.
18 x 9¾ in. (45.5 x 25 cm)
E.4481-1909.

13. Silk design by Joseph Dandridge, dated 1719.
Water colour on paper.
18¾ x 10¼ in. (47.5 x 26 cm)
E.4474-1909.

14. Design for an orrace tissue, by James Leman, date 1717.
Water colour on paper.
21½ x 11 in. (55 x 28 cm)
E.4440-1909.

15. Silk design by James Leman for "a paduasoy or tabby
tissue", dated 1719 on the back.
Water colour on paper.
21½ x 10½ in. (55 x 26.5 cm)
E.4443-1909.

16. Silk design by James Leman, dated 1719 on the back.
Water colour on paper.
24¹/₄ x 10¹/₂ in. (61.5 x 26.5 cm)
E.4449-1909.

17. Silk design by James Leman, dated 1718.
Water colour on paper.
19³/₄ x 10 in. (50 x 25.5 cm)
There are drafting instructions inscribed below.
E.4499-1909.

18. Silk design by James Leman, dated 1719.
Water colour on paper.
23 x 11 in. (58.5 x 28 cm)
E.4447-1909.

19. Woven silk. Probably Spitalfields, about 1715-20.
Brocaded in silver and gold on a damask ground.
33 x 19 in. (84 x 48.2 cm)
629-1883.

20. Woven silk. Spitalfields, about 1720.
Tabby brocaded in silver thread.
24 x 20¹/₄ in. (61 x 51.4 cm)
T.445-1977.

21. Woven silk with lace pattern in green, and with
flowers and butterflies brocaded in other colours. Spitalfields,
about 1726-28.
26 x 20 in. (66 x 50.8 cm)
T.15-1951.

22. Detail of a dress. Spitalfields, about 1725-28.
Satin ground patterned in coloured silks.
Repeat, 17¹/₂ x 10¹/₈ in. (44.5 x 25.7 cm)
T.180-1962.

23. Woven silk. Spitalfields, about 1724-26.
Extended tabby brocaded in coloured silks.
Repeat, 22³/₄ x 10 in. (57.8 x 25.5 cm)
T.18-1969.

24. Woven silk. Spitalfields, about 1728.
Lace pattern in cherry red pattern weft, with floral
details brocaded.
Repeat, 18 x 16 in. (46 x 41 cm)
T.76-1936.

25. Part of a canopy. Spitalfields, about 1726-27.
Satin ground brocaded with gold thread and details in
coloured silks.
Repeat, 25 x 11 in. (63.5 x 28 cm)
The canopy is almost certainly part of that used at the
Coronation of George II in 1727. Its construction and the
family tradition are borne out by the bill in the Lord
Chamberlain's accounts. The silk was supplied by the mercer
George Binckes.
T.184-1975.

26. Woven silk. Spitalfields, about 1728-30.
Satin ground brocaded with silver-gilt thread and
coloured silks.
Repeat, 21³/₄ x 21 in. (55 x 53 cm)
28A-1879.

27. *Chinoiserie*, silk design by Anna Maria Garthwaite.
1726-27.
Water colour on paper.
18 x 10¹/₄ in. (45.5 x 26 cm)
5970.29.

28. Design for a "lustring brocaded in silver and colours", by
James Leman, dated 1720.
Water colour on paper.
23¹/₄ x 12¹/₂ in. (59 x 31.5 cm)
E.4445-1909.

29. Silk design by Joseph Dandridge, dated 1720.
Water colour on paper.
23³/₄ x 10 in. (60.5 x 25.5 cm)
E.4510-1909.

30. Silk design by Joseph Dandridge. About 1720.
Water colour on paper.
26½ x 10 in. (67.5 x 25.5 cm)
E.4513-1909.

31. Silk design by Joseph Dandridge. Dated 1720 on the back.
Water colour on paper.
25 x 10½ in. (63.5 x 26.5 cm)
E.4442-1909.

32. Silk design by Joseph Dandridge. Dated 1720.
Water colour on paper.
24 x 10 in. (61 x 25.5 cm)
E.4518-1909.

33. Silk design by James Leman. Dated 1721.
Water colour on paper.
24¼ x 10 in. (61.5 x 25.5 cm)
E.4455-1909.

34. Silk design by James Leman. Dated 1720.
Water colour on paper.
22½ x 11 in. (57 x 28 cm)
E.4506-1909.

35. Design by James Leman for a silver lustring. Dated 1720.
Water colour on paper.
23 x 11½ in. (58.5 x 29 cm)
Also inscribed with the name of the mercer who commissioned it.
E.4507-1909.

36. Design by James Leman for a lustring brocaded with either silk or silver thread. Dated 1721.
Water colour on paper.
15½ x 10½ in. (39.5 x 26.5 cm)
E.4488-1909.

37. Silk design by James Leman. Dated 1721.
Water colour on paper.
23 x 10 in. (58.5 x 25.5 cm)
E.4519-1909.

38. Silk design, possibly by James Leman. About 1726.
Water colour on paper.
19½ X 10 in. (50 x 25.5 cm)
One of a set of "Patterns by Different Hands" which belonged to Anna Maria Garthwaite.
5973.16.

39. Silk design by Christopher Baudouin. Dated 1726 on the back.
Water colour on paper.
18½ x 9¾ in. (47 x 25 cm)
5973.1.

40. Silk design by Christopher Baudouin. About 1726.
Water colour on paper.
20¼ x 10 in. (51.5 x 25.5 cm)
5973.6.

41. Silk design by Christopher Baudouin. Dated 1724 on the back.
Water colour on paper.
24½ x 10¼ in. (62.5 x 26 cm)
5973.18.

42. Silk design by Christopher Baudouin. Dated 1725 on the back.
Water colour on paper.
22 x 10 in. (56 x 25.5 cm)
5973.15.

43. Silk design by Anna Maria Garthwaite. Dated 1728.
Water colour on paper.
23¼ x 10 in. (59 x 25.5 cm)
5970.39.

44. Silk design by Anna Maria Garthwaite. Dated 1729.
Water colour on paper.
21¾ x 10 in. (55.5 x 25.5 cm)
5970.44.

45. Detail from a dress. Spitalfields, about 1733.
Tabby ground brocaded in coloured silks and chenille.
Repeat, 22 x 10 in. (56 x 25.5 cm)
T.9-1971.

46. Silk design by Anna Maria Garthwaite. Dated 1733.
Water colour on paper.
18^1/$_2$ x 8^3/$_4$ in. (47 x 22.5 cm)
One of a set of "Double Tabbys".
5975.17.

47. Woven silk. Spitalfields or Holland, 1733.
Repeat, 18^1/$_4$ x 7^3/$_4$ in. (46.4 x 19.7 cm)
Woven after the design by Garthwaite (5975.17), or she took the
design from this silk. This is the earliest silk to come to light
which can be associated with the designs.
T.837-1974.

48. Detail from a dress. Spitalfields, about 1733.
Tabby brocaded in coloured silks and silver thread.
Repeat, 27^1/$_2$ x 10^1/$_2$ in. (70 x 26.7 cm)
T.14-1961.

49. Woven silk. Spitalfields, about 1734.
Tabby with a green pattern weft and the other
colours brocaded.
Repeat, 22 x 9^5/$_8$ in. (56 x 24.5 cm)
T.26-1966.

50. Silk damask. Spitalfields, about 1734.
Repeat, 48 x 20 in. (122 x 51 cm)
T.184-1970.

51. Woven silk. Spitalfields, about 1734.
Tabby brocaded in coloured silks.
40 x 20^3/$_4$ in. (101.6 x 52.7 cm)
This silk is worn by Mrs. Charles Broughton in her portrait
painted by Siries in 1736 (present whereabouts unknown).
T.99-1912.

52. Woven silk. Spitalfields, about 1736.
Tabby brocaded with coloured silks.
Repeat, 22^1/$_2$ x 20^3/$_4$ in. (57 x 52.7 cm)
The pattern may be compared with Plate 65.
T.35-1963.

53. Woven silk. Spitalfields, about 1741.
Tabby brocaded in colours.
23^1/$_4$ x 21 in. (59 x 53.3 cm)
1351-1871.

54. Detail from a dress. Spitalfields, about 1739-42.
Tabby brocaded in coloured silks.
Repeat, 24^1/$_2$ x 19^1/$_2$ in. (62.2 x 49.5 cm)
36-1903.

55. Detail from a dress. Spitalfields, about 1735-38.
Tabby brocaded in coloured silks.
Repeat, 18^3/$_4$ x 10^1/$_4$ in. (47.7 x 26 cm)
T.23-1972.

56. Silk design by Anna Maria Garthwaite. Dated 1738.
Water colour on paper.
25^1/$_4$ x 11^1/$_4$ in. (64 x 28.5 cm)
5977.12.

57. Silk design by Anna Maria Garthwaite. About 1730.
Water colour on paper.
19^1/$_2$ x 9 in. (50 x 23 cm)
One of a set of "Double Tabbys".
5975.2.

58. Silk design by Anna Maria Garthwaite. Dated 1731.
Water colour on paper.
23^3/$_4$ x 10 in. (60.5 x 25.5 cm)
One of a set of "Double Tabbys".
5972.3.

59. Silk design by Anna Maria Garthwaite. Dated 1732.
Water colour on paper.
24 x 10 in. (61 x 25.5 cm)
One of a set of "Gold Stuffs".
5972.4.

60. Silk design by Anna Maria Garthwaite. About 1731-32.
Water colour on paper.
23³/₄ x 9³/₄ in. (60.5 x 25 cm)
One of a set of "Double Tabbys".
5975.5.

61. Silk design by Anna Maria Garthwaite. Dated 1732.
Water colour on paper.
19¹/₄ x 8³/₄ in. (49 x 22.5 cm)
One of a set of "Double Tabbys".
5975.15.

62. Silk design by Anna Maria Garthwaite. Dated 1734.
Water colour on paper.
26¹/₄ x 10³/₄ in. (67 x 27 cm)
One of a set of "Gold Stuffs".
5972.10.

63. Silk design by Anna Maria Garthwaite. Dated 1734.
Water colour on paper.
25¹/₂ x 10³/₄ in. (65 x 27 cm)
5971.23.

64. Silk design by Anna Maria Garthwaite. Dated 1735.
Water colour on paper.
25³/₄ x 10¹/₂ in. (65.5 x 26.5 cm)
One of a set of "Brocades from 1735-40".
5977.8.

65. Silk design by Anna Maria Garthwaite. About 1736-38.
Water colour on paper.
25 x 13¹/₂ in. (63.5 x 34.5 cm)
The design may be compared with silk Plate 52.
5971.26.

66. Silk design by Anna Maria Garthwaite. Dated 1736.
Water colour on paper.
25¹/₂ x 21 in. (65 x 53.5 cm)
One of a set of "Brocades from 1735-40".
5977.5.

67. Silk design by Anna Maria Garthwaite. Dated 1738.
Water colour on paper.
25¹/₂ x 21¹/₄ in. (65 x 54 cm)
One of a set of "Brocades from 1735-40".
5977.11.

68. Woven silk. Spitalfields, about 1740.
Tabby brocaded in coloured silks.
22¹/₂ x 20¹/₂ in. (57 x 52 cm)
T.347-1910.

69. Silk design by Anna Maria Garthwaite. Dated 1742.
Water colour on paper.
14¹/₂ x 10¹/₂ in. (37 x 26.5 cm)
Inscribed with the name of the weaver, Captain Peter Lekeux,
who bought the design. The yellow is a colour code for
metal thread.
5981.20.

70. Woven silk. Spitalfields, 1742.
Taffeta brocaded in silver thread.
Repeat, 28¹/₂ x 21 in. (72.5 x 53.5 cm)
Woven by Captain Peter Lekeux from the design by Garthwaite
5981.20.
T.81-1938.

71. Woven silk. Spitalfields, about 1741-42.
Textured ground brocaded in coloured silks.
25¹/₄ x 21 in. (64 x 53.3 cm)
T.182A-1960.

72. Woven silk. Spitalfields, about 1743-45.
Taffeta brocaded in coloured silks.
23⁵/₈ x 20 in. (60 x 50.8 cm)
T.1-1970.

73. Woven silk. Spitalfields, about 1743.
Taffeta brocaded in coloured silks with a self-coloured flush
pattern in the ground.
23³/₄ x 19¹/₂ in. (60.5 x 49.5 cm)
T.423A-1977.

74. Woven silk. Spitalfields, about 1743-44.
Taffeta brocaded in silver-gilt thread and coloured silks.
Repeat, 27 x 15¹/₂ in. (68.5 x 40 cm)
T.103A-1968.

75. Design for a woven silk by Anna Maria Garthwaite.
Dated 1744.
Water colour on paper.
12¹/₂ x 10¹/₄ in. (32 x 26 cm)
The design is inscribed with the name of the weaver,
Mr. Gregory, who bought it.
5982.10.

76. Detail from a dress. Spitalfields, 1744.
Satin brocaded in coloured silks.
Repeat, 22³/₄ x 20³/₄ in. (58 x 52.7 cm)
Woven from a design by Anna Maria Garthwaite, 5982.10.
The dress was altered later in the 18th century.
T.264-1966.

77. Design for a brocaded damask by Anna Maria Garthwaite.
Dated 1744.
Water colour on paper.
13 x 10³/₈ in. (33 x 26.3 cm)
The design is inscribed with the name of the weaver, Captain
John Baker, to whom it was sold.
T.393-1971, p.9.

78. Detail from a dress. Spitalfields, 1744.
Damask brocaded in coloured silks with an additional flush
effect in the ground.
Repeat, 24 x 20¹/₂ in. (61 x 52 cm)
The silk was woven by Captain John Baker from the design by
Anna Maria Garthwaite, T.393-1971, p.9.
Circ.85-1951.

79. Woven silk. Spitalfields, about 1742-43.
Tabby brocaded with coloured silks.
Repeat, 21³/₄ x 19 in. (55.2 x 48.3 cm)
T.45-1968.

80. Woven silk. Spitalfields, about 1747-50.
Tabby with tobine stripes, brocaded with coloured silks.
24 x 20 in. (61 x 50.8 cm)
T.138-1963.

81. Woven silk, *Rocaille*. Spitalfields, about 1745.
Tabby brocaded with silks and silver thread.
Repeat, 30³/₄ x 20¹/₄ in. (78 x 51.4 cm)
T.296-1975.

82. Design for a "bro[caded] lut[estring] one shade" by Anna
Maria Garthwaite. Dated 1745.
Water colour on paper. 14¹/₂ x 10¹/₄ in. (37 x 26 cm)
The design is inscribed with the name of the weaver, Daniel(?)
Vautier, to whom it was sold. It may be compared with T.296-
1975, Plate 81.
5983.22.

83. Woven silk. Spitalfields, about 1746.
Tabby with two broad satin stripes and flowers, brocaded in
coloured silks.
Repeat, 26³/₈ x 20³/₄ in. (67 x 52.7 cm)
T.257-1973.

84. Woven silk. Spitalfields, about 1747-49.
Tabby brocaded with coloured silks, with a flush pattern
in the ground.
Repeat, 33¹/₂ x 15 in. (85 x 38 cm)
T. 77-1924.

85. Woven silk. Spitalfields, about 1749.
Tabby brocaded with coloured silks, with a flush pattern
in the ground.
30 x 20³/₄ in. (76.2 x 52.7 cm)
T.146-1973.

86. Design for a "bro[caded] tobine" by Anna Maria
Garthwaite. Dated 1747.
Water colour on paper.
14³/₄ x 9³/₄ in. (37.5 x 24.7 cm)
The design is also inscribed with the name of the weaver,
Daniel(?) Vautier, to whom it was sold.
5985.2.

87. Detail from a dress. Spitalfields, 1747.
Tabby brocaded in coloured silks with a self-coloured tobine or *cannelé* pattern.
Repeat, 17 x 10 in. (43.2 x 25.5 cm)
The silk was woven from the design by Anna Maria Garthwaite, 5985.2, by Daniel(?) Vautier in 1747. The dress has been altered later.
T.706-1913.

88. Woven silk. Spitalfields, about 1747-49.
Satin brocaded in coloured silks.
Repeat, 25 x 20¹/₂ in. (63.5 x 52 cm)
606-1906.

89. Woven silk. Spitalfields, about 1749-50.
Satin brocaded in coloured silks.
25¹/₄ x 20¹/₂ in. (64 x 52 cm)
In the style of John Vansommer.
T.353-1960.

90. Design for a "bro[caded] lut[estring] " by Anna Maria Garthwaite . Dated 1747.
Water colour on paper.
20³/₄ x 10¹/₂ in. (52.5 x 26.5 cm)
The design is also inscribed with the name of the weaver, Daniel(?) Vautier, to whom it was sold.
5985.9.

91. Detail from a dress. Spitalfields, 1747.
Brocaded lustring.
Repeat, 18 x 20¹/₂ in. (45.8 x 52 cm)
Woven by Daniel(?) Vautier from the design by Anna Maria Garthwaite, 5985.9, dated 1747.
T.720-1913.

92. Design for a "bro[caded] lut[estring]" by Anna Maria Garthwaite. Dated 1748.
Water colour on paper.
15¹/₄ x 10³/₄ in. (38.5 x 27.5 cm)
The design is inscribed with the name of the weaver, "Mr. Brant", to whom it was sold.
5986.8.

93. Woven silk. Spitalfields, 1748.
Tabby with an additional flush pattern brocaded with coloured silks.
27³/₄ x 19 in. (70.5 x 48.2 cm)
Woven by Thomas Brant from the design by Anna Maria Garthwaite, 5986.8. He has changed the lustring to a heavier material, added the pattern in the ground and changed the colour of the main branch.
T.177-1961.

94. Musical trophies and Union Jacks, woven silk. Spitalfields, about 1743-49.
Textured ground brocaded in coloured silks.
Repeat, 23¹/₂ x 20¹/₂ in. (60 x 52 cm)
The silk was probably specially woven, but the occasion has not so far been identified.
T.171-1965.

95. Detail from a dress. Spitalfields, about 1749.
Textured ground brocaded in coloured silks.
Repeat, 13¹/₂ x 9¹/₂ in. (34.3 x 24.1 cm)
124-1901.

96. Woven silk. Spitalfields, about 1746-49.
Tabby brocaded with coloured silks, with an additional flush pattern in the ground.
Repeat, 31 x 19³/₄ in. (78.8 x 50.2 cm)
T.395-1977.

97. Worsted. Norwich, about 1725-50.
Damask brocaded with coloured worsteds.
Repeat, 21³/₄ x 17³/₄ in. (55.5 x 45 cm)
T.288-1962.

98. Worsted. Norwich, mid 18th century.
Damask brocaded in colours.
Repeat, 21¹/₂ x 17³/₄ in. (54.5 x 45 cm)
T.142-1962.

99. Woven silk. Spitalfields, 1740.
Tabby brocaded with coloured silks.
23¹/₄ x 20¹/₂ in. (59.5 x 52 cm)
The silk was woven from the design by Anna Maria Garthwaite
5981.8a, by Captain Peter Lekeux.
T.219-1989.

100. Silk design by Anna Maria Garthwaite. Dated 1740.
Water colour on paper.
13¹/₄ x 10³/₄ in. (33.5 x 27.5 cm)
The design bears the name of the weaver to whom it was sold,
Captain Peter Lekeux. Three silks woven from this design have
survived, of which one is in the Royal Ontario Museum,
Toronto, 968.36.1. and another illustrated plate 99.
5981.8a.

101. Silk design by Anna Maria Garthwaite. Dated 1741.
Water colour on paper.
13¹/₄ x 10¹/₄ in. (33.5 x 26 cm)
One of a set of patterns "Tobines in 1741". These are warp-
patterned silks; hence the vertical stripes.
5978.9.

102-107. Silk designs by Anna Maria Garthwaite. Dated 1741.
Water colour on paper.
18 x 11¹/₂ in. (46 x 29 cm)
Although from the set of "Tobines in 1741" two of the patterns
are velvets for men's suitings, and one is a grogram, i.e. a half
silk, also a suiting. One of the tobines is on point-paper from
which the pattern can be entered on the loom.
5978.13.

108. Design for brocaded silk (?) by Anna Maria
Garthwaite. 1741.
Water colour on paper.
26¹/₄ x 20³/₄ in. (66.5 x 53 cm)
From a set of "Patterns in 1741".
5979.6.

109. Design for brocaded silk (?) by Anna Maria
Garthwaite. 1742.
Water colour on paper.
29³/₄ x 20³/₄ in. (75 x 52.5 cm)
From a set of "Patterns drawn in 1742".
5980.7.

110. Silk design by Anna Maria Garthwaite. About 1740.
Water colour on paper.
28¹/₄ x 21¹/₄ in. (72 x 54 cm)
One of a set of "Double Tabbys".
5975.22.

111. Silk design by Anna Maria Garthwaite. Dated 1742.
Water colour on paper.
14³/₄ x 10¹/₂ in. (37.5 x 26.5 cm)
Inscribed with the name of the weaver, Captain Peter Lekeux,
who bought the design. This would have been woven in
metal thread (for which the yellow is a colour code) and
brocaded silks.
5981.13.

112. Design for a tissue by Anna Maria Garthwaite. Dated 1742.
Water colour on paper.
12¹/₄ x 10¹/₄ in. (31 x 26 cm)
Inscribed with the name of the weaver, Captain John Baker,
who bought the design.
5981.23.

113. "Holly Leaves", design for a brocaded tabby by Anna Maria
Garthwaite. Dated 1743.
Water colour on paper.
15 x 10¹/₄ in. (38 x 26 cm)
Inscribed with the name of the mercers, Palmer & Halsey
of Ludgate Hill, who commissioned it, and the weaver,
Daniel(?) Vautier.
T.392-1971, p.31.

114. Design for "a silver lut[estring]" by Anna Maria
Garthwaite. Dated 1743.
Water colour on paper.
20³/₄ x 10¹/₄ in. (52.5 x 26 cm)
Inscribed with the name of the weaver, Daniel Gobbé, and the
mercer who commissioned it, Robert Carr of Ludgate Hill.
T.391-1971, p.83.

115. "Aloe leaf", design for a brocaded tabby by Anna Maria
Garthwaite. Dated 1743.
Water colour on paper.
21 x 10¹/₄ in. (53 x 26 cm)
Inscribed with the name of the weaver, Daniel Gobbé, to whom
it was sold.
T.391-1971, p.37.

116. Design for a "Bro[caded] lut[estring] gimp ground" by
Anna Maria Garthwaite. Dated 1743.
Water colour on paper.
12¹/₄ x 10 in. (31 x 25.5 cm)
Inscribed with the name of the weaver, Mr. Gregory, to whom
it was sold. "Gimp" is a thick thread and it is difficult to
visualise its use in such a material.
T.392-1971, p.53.

117. Design for a "Bro[caded] tabby India" by Anna Maria
Garthwaite. Dated 1743.
Water colour on paper.
15¹/₄ x 10¹/₂ in. (38.5 x 26.5 cm)
Inscribed with the name of the weaver, Daniel(?) Vautier, and
the mercers, Palmer and Halsey of Ludgate Hill, who
commissioned it.
T.392-1971, p.17.

118. Design for a tobine by Anna Maria Garthwaite.
Dated 1744.
Water colour on paper.
17¹/₂ x 10¹/₄ in. (44.5 x 26 cm)
Inscribed with the name of the weaver, Daniel(?) Vautier, and
the mercer, Philip Palmer of Palmer & Halsey of Ludgate Hill,
who commissioned it.
5982.26.

119. Design for a "Bro[caded] lut[estring]" by Anna Maria
Garthwaite. Dated 1743.
Water colour on paper.
14¹/₂ x 10¹/₄ in. (37 x 26 cm)
Inscribed with the name of the weaver, Daniel Gobbé, and the
mercer, Robert Carr of Ludgate Hill, who commissioned it.
T.391-1971, p.107.

120. Design for a "Bro[caded] dam[ask]" by Anna Maria
Garthwaite. Dated 1744.
Water colour on paper.
17 x 10¹/₂ in. (43 x 26.5 cm)
Inscribed with the name of the mercer who commissioned it,
Philip Palmer of Palmer & Halsey of Ludgate Hill.
T.393-1971, p.2.

121. Design for a "Bro[caded] dam[ask]" by Anna Maria
Garthwaite. Dated 1744.
Water colour on paper.
13 x 10¹/₄ in. (33 x 26 cm)
Inscribed with the name of the weaver, Daniel(?) Vautier;
according to the index of designs for that year commissioned
by Robert Carr of Ludgate Hill.
5982.11.

122. Design for a "Bro[caded] lut[estring]" by Anna Maria
Garthwaite. Dated 1744.
Water colour on paper.
14³/₄ x 10¹/₂ in. (37.5 x 26.5 cm)
Inscribed with the name of the weaver, Captain John Baker, to
whom it was sold.
T.393-1971, p.16.

123. Design for a "Bro[cade] one shade" by Anna Maria
Garthwaite. Dated 1745.
Water colour on paper.
14¹/₂ x 10¹/₂ in. (37 x 26.5 cm)
Inscribed with the name of the weaver, Daniel(?) Vautier,
and the mercer, Miles Halsey, partner of Philip Palmer of
Ludgate Hill.
5983.11.

124. Design for a "Bro[caded] satin" by Anna Maria Garthwaite.
Dated 1745.
Water colour on paper.
12$^1/_2$ x 10$^1/_2$ in. (31.5 x 26.5 cm)
Inscribed with the name of the weaver Mr Gregory, to whom it was sold.
5983.3.

125. Design for a "Bro[caded] lut[estring]" by Anna Maria Garthwaite. Dated 1747.
Water colour on paper.
10$^3/_4$ x 10$^3/_4$ in. (27 x 27 cm)
Inscribed with the name of the weaver, Daniel(?) Vautier, to whom it was sold.
5985.3.

126. Design for a "Bro[caded] Tis[sue]" by Anna Maria Garthwaite. Dated 1747.
Water colour on paper.
13$^1/_2$ x 10$^3/_4$ in. (34.5 x 27 cm)
Inscribed with the name of the weaver, James Godin, to whom it was sold.
5985.1.

127. Design for a "Brocaded Tobine" by Anna Maria Garthwaite. Dated 1749.
Water colour on paper.
14$^3/_4$ x 10 in. (37.5 x 25.5 cm)

Inscribed with the name of the weaver, Daniel(?) Vautier, to whom it was sold.
5987.1.

128. Design for a "Bro[cade] Tobine Ground" by Anna Maria Garthwaite . Dated 1748.
Water colour on paper.
9 x 5 in. (23 x 13 cm)
Inscribed with the name of the weaver, Daniel(?) Vautier, to whom it was sold.
5986.3.

129. Four designs for "Tobines" by Anna Maria Garthwaite. Dated 1749.
Water colour on paper.
18 x 11$^1/_4$ in. (45.5 x 28.5 cm)
Inscribed with the names of the weavers to whom they were sold, probably John Chaplin and two members of the Mase family.
5987.13.

130. Design for a "Bro[cade]d flow[ere]d tabby" by Anna Maria Garthwaite . Dated 1749.
Water colour on paper.
12$^3/_4$ x 5$^1/_4$ in. (32.5 x 13 cm)
Inscribed with the name of the weaver, probably John Luke Landon, to whom it was sold.
5987.3.

1: Woven silk. Probably English, third quarter 17th century. T.14-1922

2: Worsted damask. Norwich or Spitalfields, about 1720-30. T.675-1974

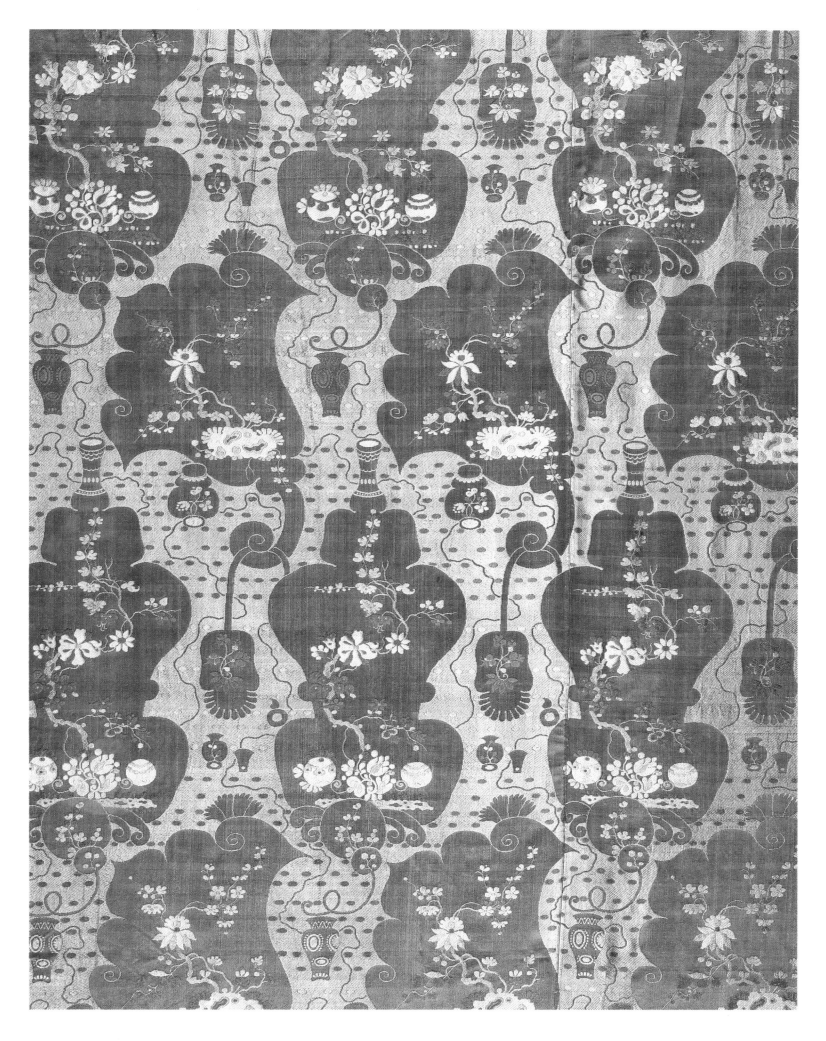

3: Woven silk. Spitalfields or Holland, about 1709. T.173-1965

4: Woven silk. Spitalfields, about 1707-08. 711-1864

5: Christening blanket. Spitalfields or Holland, about 1711-12. T.225-1973

6: Woven silk. Spitalfields, about 1712-15. T.148A-1968

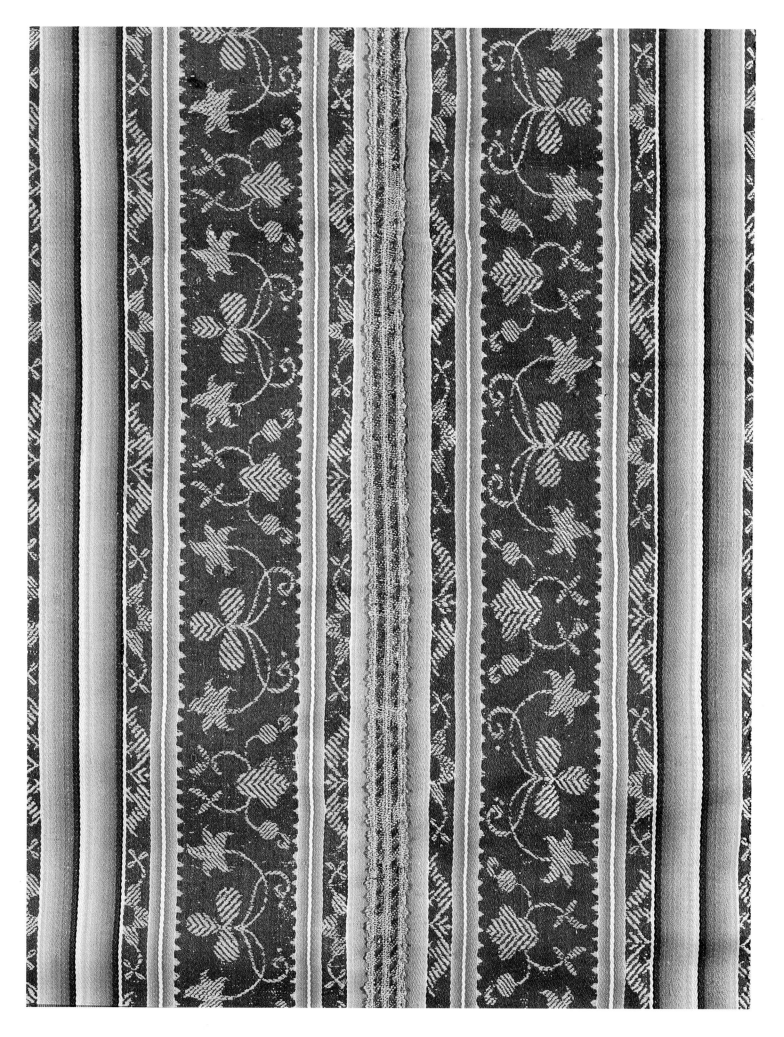

7: Worsted. Norwich or Spitalfields, early 18th century. T.287-1962

8: Silk design by Joseph Dandridge. Dated 1718. E.4466-1909

9: Silk design by James Leman. Dated 1721. E.4450-1909

10: Silk design by James Leman. Dated 1718. E.4465-1909

May 11th 1719 // 400 cords No 8 & 10 — Dezines tinyr

for Mr Tullie —

Mr Dandridge please to finish some of this pattern as soon as may

11: Silk design by Joseph Dandridge. Dated 1719. E.4471-1909

L N8 1

12: Silk design by James Leman. About 1717. E.4481-1909

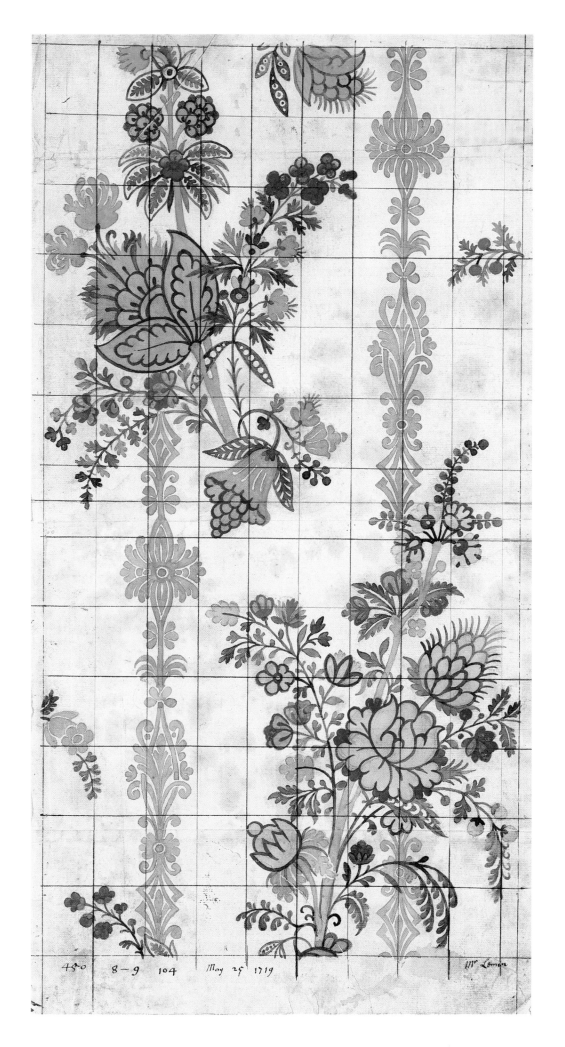

450   8—9   104   May 25 1719   Mr Lamon

13: Silk design by Joseph Dandridge. Dated 1719. E4474-1909

14: Silk design by James Leman. Dated 1717. E.4440-1909

15

16

46

17

18

19: Silk brocaded in gold and silver. Probably Spitalfields, about 1715-20. 629-1883

20: Silk brocaded in silver thread. Spitalfields, about 1720. T.445-1977

21: Brocaded silk. Spitalfields, about 1726-28. T.15-1951

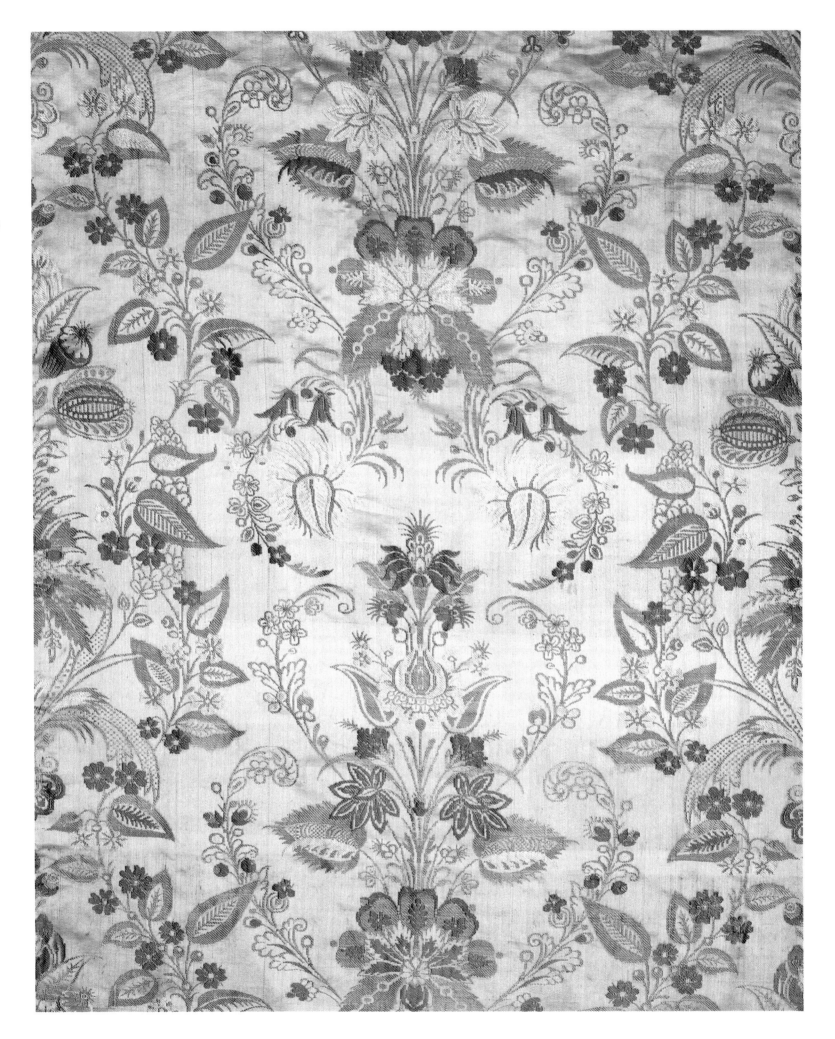

22: Woven silk, Spitalfields, about 1725-28. T.180-1962

23: Woven silk. Spitalfields, about 1724-26. T.18-1969

24: Woven silk. Spitalfields, about 1728. T.76-1936

25: Part of Coronation canopy of George II. Spitalfields, about 1726-27. T.184-1975

54

26: Woven silk. Spitalfields, about 1728-30. 28A-1879

27: Silk design by Anna Maria Garthwaite. About 1726-27. 5970-29

28: Silk design by James Leman. Dated 1720. E.4445-1909

29

30

58

31

32

33

34

60

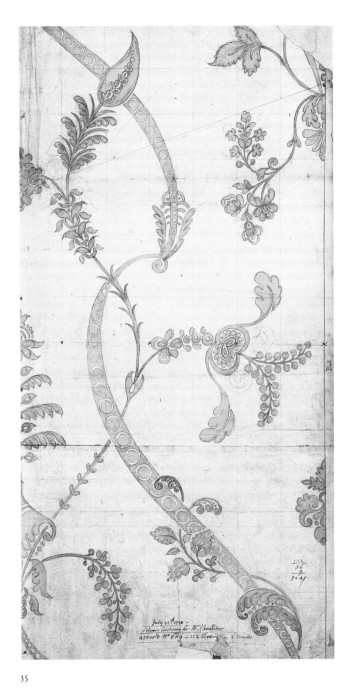

35

36

61

37

38

62

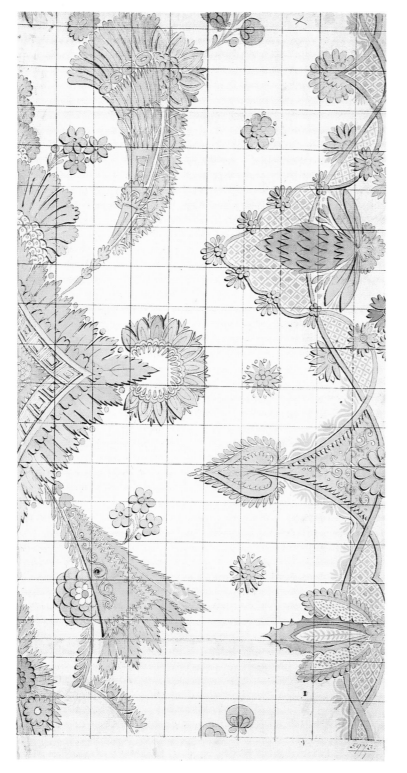

39

40

41

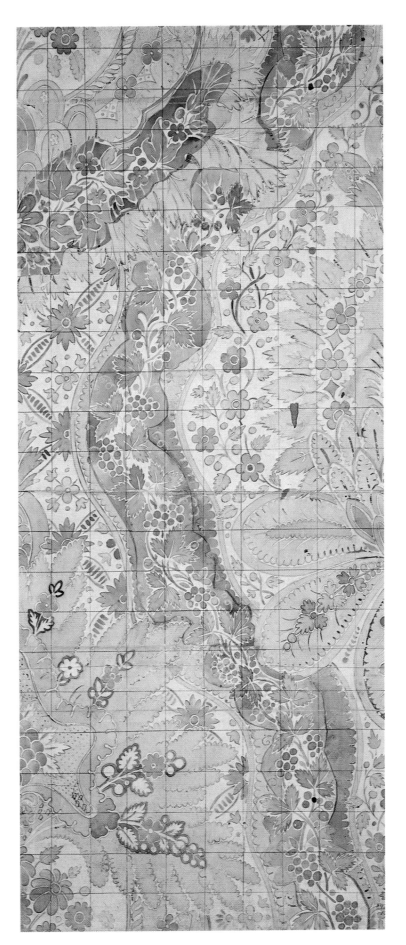

42

42: Silk design by Christopher Baudouin. Dated 1725. 5973.15

64

43

44

45: Brocaded silk. Spitalfield, about 1733. T.9-1971

46: Silk design by Anna Maria Garthwaite. Dated 1733. 5875.17

47: Woven silk. Spitalfields or Holland, 1733. T.837-1974

68

48: Brocaded silk. Spitalfields, about 1733. T.14-1961

49

50

51: Woven silk. Spitalfields, about 1734. T.99-1912

52: Woven silk. Spitalfields, about 1736. T.35-1963

71

52

53

54: Brocaded silk. Spitalfields, about 1739-42. 36-1903

55: Brocaded silk. Spitalfields, about 1735-38. T.23-1972

74

56

57

58

59

76

60

61

62

63

63: Silk design by Anna Maria Garthwaite. Dated 1734. 5971.23

78

64

65

66: Silk design by Anna Maria Garthwaite. Dated 1736. 5977.5

67: Silk design by Anna Maria Garthwaite. Dated 1738. 5977.11

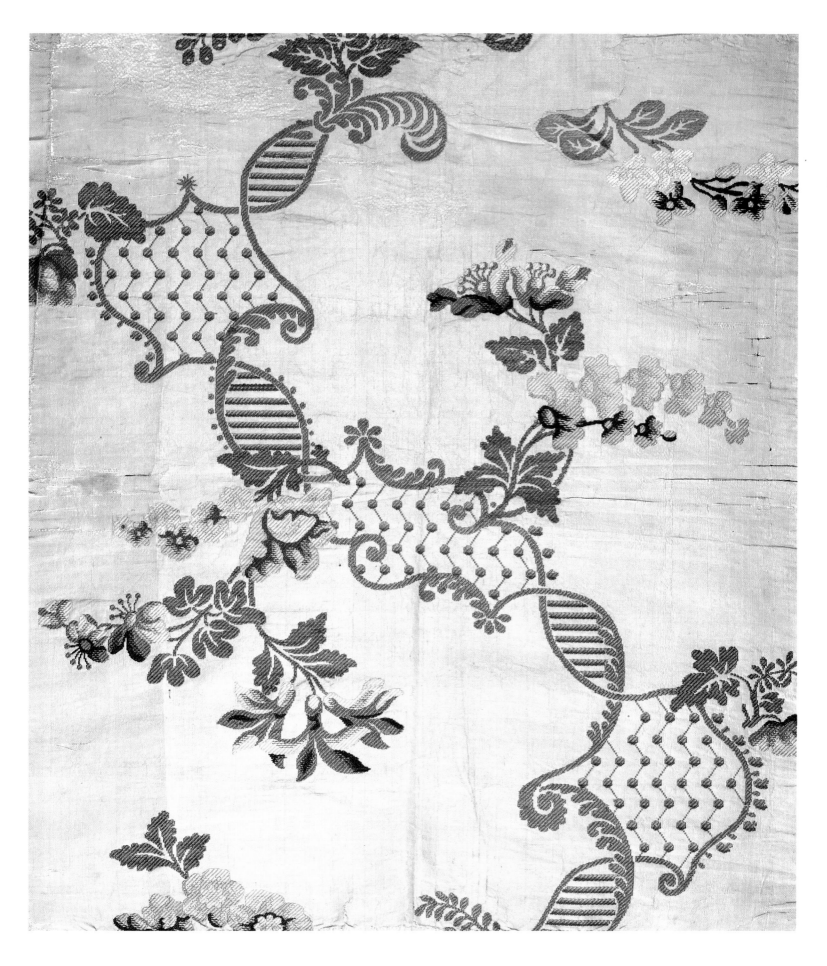

68: Brocaded silk. Spitalfields, about 1740. T.347-1910

82

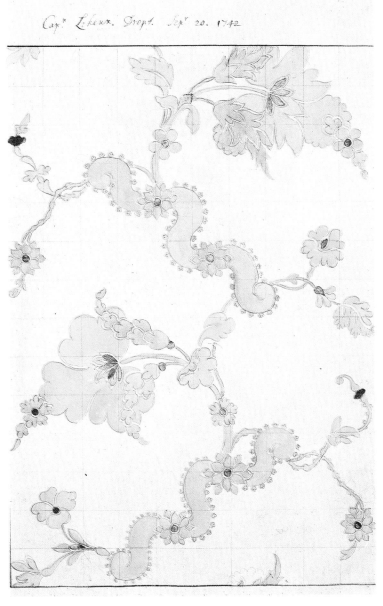

69

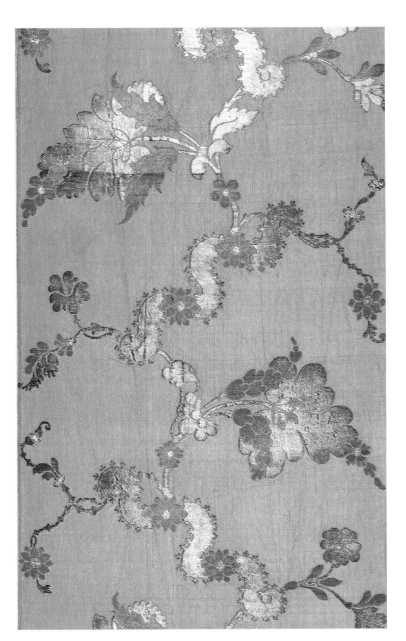

70

71: Brocaded silk. Spitalfields, about 1741-42. T.182A-1960

72: Brocaded silk. Spitalfields, about 1743-45. T.1-1970

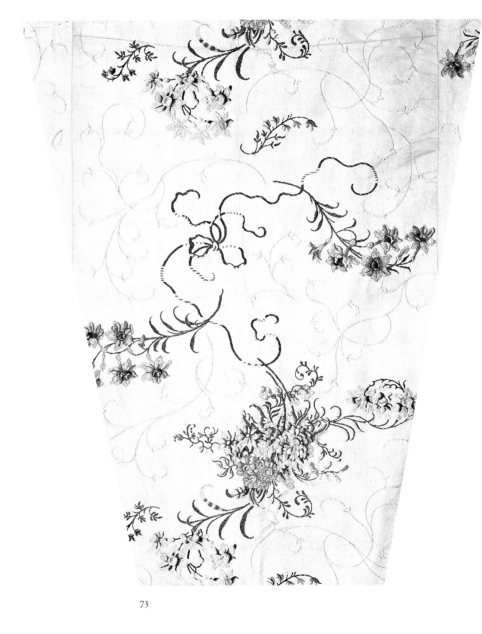

73

74

86

1111.4

75: Silk design by Anna Maria Garthwaite. Dated 1744. 5982.10

76: Brocaded silk. Spitalfields, 1744. T.264-1966

Cap.ⁿ Baker. May 12. 1744

77: Silk design by Anna Maria Garthwaite. Dated 1744. T.393-1971 p.9

78: Brocaded silk damask, Spitalfields, 1744. Circ.85-1951

79: Woven silk. Spitalfields, about 1742-43. T.45-1968

80: Brocaded silk. Spitalfields, about 1747-50. T.138-1963

92

81

82

83: Woven silk. Spitalfields, about 1746. T.257-1973

94

84: Woven silk. Spitalfields, about 1747-49. T.77-1924

85: Woven silk. Spitalfields, about 1749. T.146-1973

86: Silk design by Anna Maria Garthwaite. Dated 1747. 5985.2

87: Brocaded silk. Woven by Daniel (?) Vautier, 1747. T.706-1913

88: Woven silk. Spitalfields, about 1747-9. 606-1906

89: Woven silk. Spitalfields, about 1749-50. T.353-1960

100

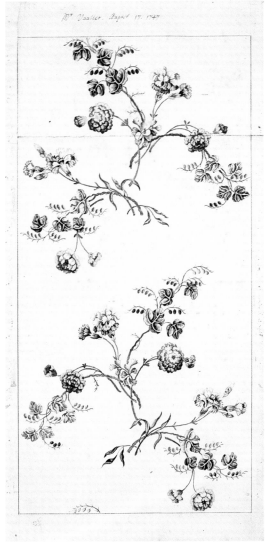

90

91

92

93

102

94

95

96: Woven silk, Spitalfields, about 1746-49. T.395-1977

104

97: Brocaded worsted damask. Norwich, about 1725-50. T.288-1962

98: Brocaded worsted damask. Norwich, mid 18th century. T.142-1962

99. Woven silk. Spitalfields, 1740. T.219-1989

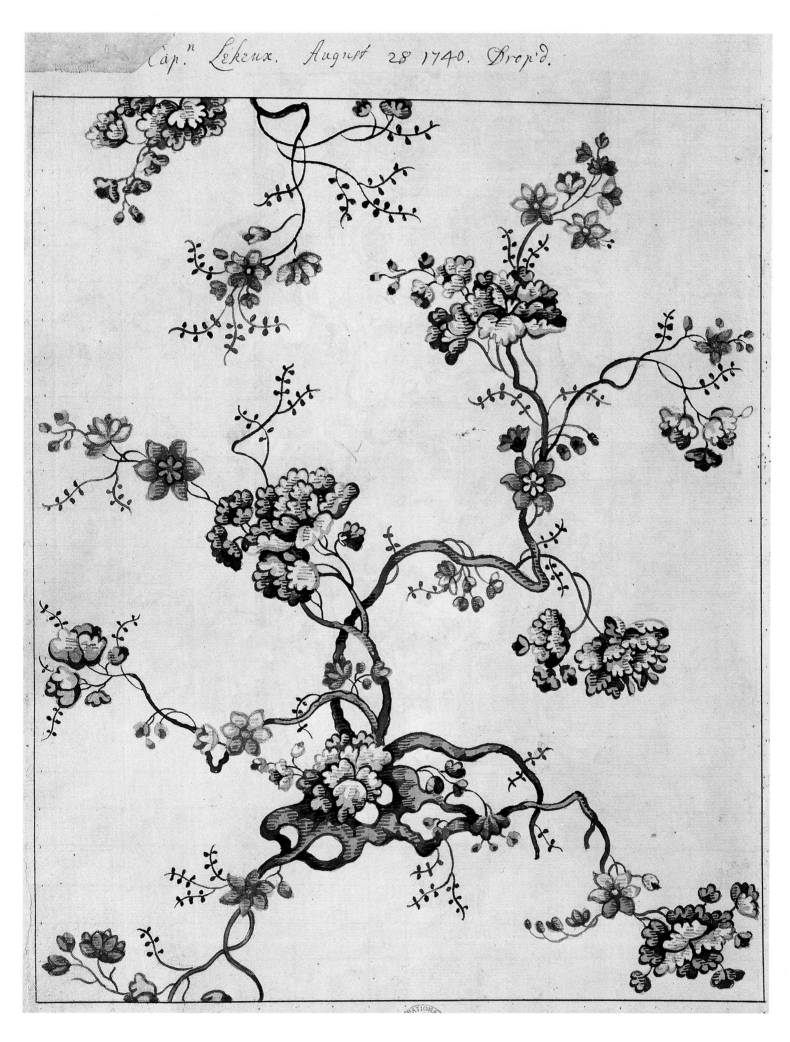

Cap.ⁿ Lekeux. August 28 1740. Drop'd.

100: Silk design by Anna Maria Garthwaite. Dated 1740. 5981.8a

108

101

102 - 107

108

109

108: Silk design by Anna Maria Garthwaite, 1741. 5979.6
109: Silk design by Anna Maria Garthwaite, 1742. 5980.7

110: Silk design by Anna Maria Garthwaite. About 1740. 5975.22

110

Capt. Lebuix. July 8 1742.

111

Capt. Baker. Nov.r 4. 1742. Point & Com. A Tissue. 1 Shuttle ½ Bro.

112

113: Silk design by Anna Maria Garthwaite. Dated 1743. T.392-1971 p.13

112

114

115

113

116

117

118

119

118: Silk design by Anna Maria Garthwaite. Dated 1744. 5982.26
119: Silk design by Anna Maria Garthwaite. Dated 1743. T.391-1971 p.107

114

120: Silk design by Anna Maria Garthwaite. Dated 1744. T.393-1971 p.2

Mr Vanteir. Aprill 24. 1744

121: Silk design by Anna Maria Garthwaite. Dated 1744. 5982.11

116

122

123

124

125

126

127

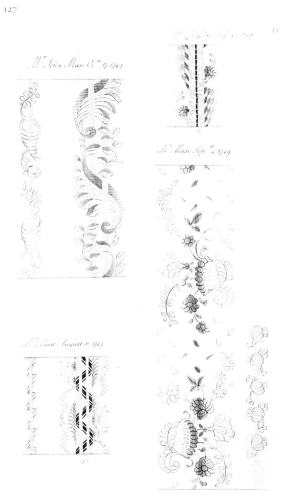

128

129

128: Silk design by Anna Maria Garthwaite. Dated 1748. 5986.3
129: Silk designs by Anna Maria Garthwaite. Dated 1749. 5987.13

130: Silk design by Anna Maria Garthwaite. Dated 1749. 5987.3

GLOSSARY

BEARING MANTLE   See CHRISTENING BLANKET.

BROCADE   The term was used in the 18th century in a strict technical sense for a brocaded silk, one in which the wefts making the pattern are only carried across the width of the motif.

BROCADING   (i) The action of the weaver in carrying the brocaded weft across one limited section of the warp. (ii) The area in the textile which has been brocaded. When silk and, still more, metal thread were much more expensive than labour, it was economic to make a woven pattern by this method.

CAMLET   A fine worsted used for both clothing and furnishings. Its weave was tabby, but it could have mohair or silk added to improve the quality. This was an important material throughout the later 17th and the whole of the 18th century.

CANOPY   As part of the British Coronation ceremony an elaborate cover was constructed to carry over the new King as he walked in procession. This was made of silks which matched the Coronation Chair, etc. Such objects became the perquisites of certain officials.

CHASUBLE   Principal vestment worn by the priest for the celebration of the Mass. Medieval chasubles were originally of more or less conical form.

CHENILLE   This is a thread, in use from the late 17th century, which is in the form of a furry cord – rather like a caterpillar, hence its name. It is made by weaving a material in which the warp threads are arranged in groups of 2 to 6 ends which interlace like gauze, the groups being a definite distance apart to suit the length of the pile. The weft is inserted in the normal way, each shoot representing a potential tuft. The woven piece is cut into warpwise strips, which are then used as weft yarn.

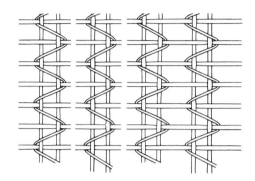

CHINOISERIE   The European idea of Chinese decoration, inspired by many disparate objects, which were often not Chinese. The style of *chinoiserie* changed with the different aesthetic movements, but it was essentially an excuse for exotic fanciful decoration.

CHRISTENING BLANKET   Part of the ceremonial equipment used at christenings. It was generally a very high quality material, trimmed with lace, on which the baby was carried to the font to be baptised. The baby's clothes were made to match and the whole set kept in a basket lined with the same material. Since the outfit was only used once in a baby's life, several very fine sets have survived from the 17th and 18th centuries. Often the blanket alone has survived.

CLOUDS   Silks printed on the warp before weaving were called "clouds" in England and *chiné* in France. They were specially fashionable in the second half of the 18th century. When woven, the colour printed on the warp is muted by the uncoloured weft, hence the name.

COMBER   The term is used by 18th century designers in several senses: (i) a straight repeat i.e. / / / / (ii) a complete repeat horizontally. The number of repeats in the width was determined by the comber-board. The cords making the pattern were threaded through this at the top of the loom. The board could be divided into sections each one constituting a repeat. The cords for the same part of the design in each repeat were then tied together at the neck of the pulley. Many of the silks and designs of the period up to the mid 1760s were "single comber" with only one repeat in the width of the textile. The journeymen charged more for such designs in their List of Prices of 1769.

CORDS The inscriptions on Leman's designs specifying "400 cords", for example, meant that the design must be spaced out horizontally over 400 units and the draft on "ruled paper" had to be prepared accordingly. The cords are those tied together at the neck of the pulley and controlled by the lashes on the simple.

CUT AND UNCUT VELVET Velvet (see below) with part of the pile left uncut and other details cut. The material was often used for men's suitings.

DAMASK A patterned textile with one warp and one weft in which the design is formed by a contrast of binding systems. In its classic form it is reversible and the contrast is produced by the warp and weft faces of the same weave. By extension two distinct binding systems may also be employed. (Definition from CIETA Vocabulary.) In a damask the warp and weft face of the same weave appeared side by side. Damasks were usually based upon satin, but this was not essential. Their patterns "require the boldest stroke of any; the flowers and leaves should always be large and the small work omitted as much as possible except it be in the middle of a flower...a bold stroke with the line of beauty and well shaped stalks leafs and flowers natural or imaginary, are the only things a designer has to observe in the compleating of a well designed damask pattern" *(Laboratory, p.42)*. Their designs sometimes lagged a little behind those of polychrome silks. When Mrs. Charles Willing sat to Robert Feke in 1746 she was wearing a damask designed by Garthwaite in 1743. They had very long repeats; plate 50 is 48 inches, the full length of a sack-back dress.

DEZINE Unit of measurement for the length of a pattern. It was often abbreviated to "dez" by James Leman and "duz" by Joseph Dandridge. The dezines are subdivided according to the size of the paper to be used for the draft, usually into 8 or 10 small squares, each representing one line in the pattern.

DIAPER All-over pattern of diamond-shapes used in embroidery and in some woven fabrics.

DOUBLE TABBY This had a tabby ground with a pattern, usually in the same colour, bound in twill by a proportion of the threads of the ground warp. It was a substantial material. A *paduasoy* (q.v.) may have been a virtually identical material when it was patterned. See also TABBY.

DROPT The term refers to the repeat of the design. A dropped repeat is one in which the design unit is moved horizontally half the width of the repeat and dropped vertically the length of the full repeat (CIETA definition). Most of the designs by Garthwaite described as "dropped" are actually drop reverse designs; i.e. the design unit is reversed horizontally and dropped. Moreover she also used the word quite loosely, since sometimes the two halves are not identical, e.g. Plates 69 and 70.

FIGURE, FIGURED The term was used by 18th century designers for both the whole pattern and part of it. "Figured" was used loosely for "patterned".

FLOUNCE A term used for the band of decoration at the hem of a dress. This could be woven, printed or embroidered – or simply an extra frill of material.

FLUSH A design effect formed by an unbound weft, either a pattern weft (passing from selvage to selvage and additional to the ground weft) or a ground weft. N.B. modern CIETA usage confines the word to warp effects whereas it was a term only applied to weft effects in the 18th century. It is frequently found as a subsidiary to other effects. The journeymen weavers charged extra for this in their wages agreement of 1769. List of Prices Foot-Figured and Flowered, p.7, No.1, Half ell plain and figured Mantuas per yard. "For a *flush* out of the ground 12 figured treadles to 16 figured lambs or under...3d." p.14, No.8, Single tissues 5 threads in the reed "a flush made with the ground shuttle...6d...if with an additional flush per yard...1.3d."

FOOT-FIGURED   These are patterns made not on a drawloom but with multiple shafts. Their designs are either geometric or on a very small scale, since there was a practical limit to the number of shafts.

FROST (FRISÉ)   A metal or silk thread in which one component is twisted more tightly than the other to produce a bumpy effect. When carried out in metal thread this gives an additional sparkle.

GAUZE   A weave with a twisted warp. The loom contains a shaft which can be moved sideways and this carries the "doup" ends alternately to the right or left of fixed ends. There are many variations, according to the complexity of the movements made by the doup ends in relation to the fixed ones.

GROGRAM   This was a half silk, often with a silk warp and a worsted weft. The material was much cheaper than pure silk and a common one for men's suitings. When Garthwaite drew a pattern for a waistcoat "shape" in grogram she did not do a pocket flap as she would have done for pure silk.

INSTRUCTIONS FOR DRAFTING   Many of the silk designs illustrated bear instructions, e.g. plate 17, "450 cords no 10 & 10, 88 dezines" and in this instance also instructions for painting several colours together in one line. From these details the draftsman could prepare the "rule paper" or point-paper from which the loom was entered. 10 & 10 is the count of the paper, 10 squares in each direction within each dezine (CORDS and DEZINE, see above).

JAPONAISERIE   Japanese porcelain and lacquer inspired in the European mind a set of decorative ideas slightly different from those of *chinoiserie*. Plate 3 is a good example.

JOURNEYMAN WEAVER   The name of the journeyman weaver who was to weave the silk was noted on his designs by James Leman. Batchelor, Ham and Perigal also wrote the name of the journeyman who was to weave a particular silk on the sample. Journeymen worked in their own homes for the master weavers.

LUSTRING (LUTESTRING)   This was closely woven, very lightweight tabby with an extra sheen imparted by a special process by which the warp was heated and stretched after being coated with beer or something similar. In order to show off this ground "the design must be open and airy composed of various sorts of flowers carelessly disposed and garnished" *(Laboratory, p.41)*. The material was produced from the late 17th to the early 19th century. Some of the most successful English silks were lustrings and it was a favourite export to the American colonies. Although first produced as a black silk exclusively by the Royal Lustring Company, by the time the Company was dissolved in 1718 it had become one of the standard dress materials and remained so until the last quarter of the century.

MASTER WEAVER   James Leman, together with most of the names on the Garthwaite designs, and the firm of Batchelor, Ham and Perigal, are all master weavers. Some of the richest might produce goods for sale to the mercers each season but, increasingly, they received commissions for work and then gave it out to their journeymen. The latter were given a warp and a draft from which to enter the pattern. James Leman was unusual in, apparently, having a workshop as well as giving out work.

MERCER   The master weavers sought orders for their goods from the retailers, the mercers of Ludgate Hill and Covent Garden. These men sold only silks and high quality worsteds. Garthwaite lists their names together with that of the master weaver to whom she sold her designs and their names are also inscribed on the samples of the weavers Batchelor, Ham and Perigal. The samples for each season were shown to the mercer who then placed his orders. The silk was then woven by the journeyman weaver as instructed and both names written on the sample.

MONTURE (MOUNTURE)   Drawloom.

NUMERALS   Apart from instructions for drafting (see above), on some designs there are listed the number of threads in each portee. These figures are sometimes at the foot of the design, sometimes written on stripes, etc.

ORRACE TISSUE A tissue (q.v.) which was probably chiefly or exclusively metal thread. James Leman's design, plate 14, was probably for the latter, since it is painted in a single wash like the damask designs.

PADUASOY Possibly the heaviest silk tabby on sale in the 18th century. When patterned, it had an additional binding warp and may be the same, technically, as a double tabby and a tabby tissue. Leman's design, plate 15, is for such a material. It was expensive, since it used much high quality silk. Smith explained in the *Laboratory*, p.41, "paduasoy and double ground brocades require a grand look...sometimes the brocades are worked on a Paduasoy double tissue, the colour of the figure whereof is commonly that of the ground".

PATTERN WEFT A pattern weft, unlike a brocaded weft, is taken from selvage to selvage by the weaver. The 18th century term was probably "backshoot".

POINT A term referring to the type of repeat. A point design produces a symmetrical pattern, since the last cords of the comber unit are tied at the neck of the pulley to the first of the next. Garthwaite occasionally states that a design is to be "point and comber". The design would repeat thus: ╱╲╱╲

POINT PAPER The paper on to which the design was transferred for reading into the loom. The term used by 18th century designers was Rule Paper or "R.P." It was divided like modern graph paper into large squares and then further subdivided into smaller ones according to the different counts, e.g. 8 horizontally and 10 vertically, or 10 & 10, etc. Different proportions were used for different kinds of textile. The designer had to be familiar with these or his pattern would come out either squashed or elongated. An example of "rule paper" appears on plate 107. A well known brand of early 19th century paper carried as a trade-mark the name "Anna Maria Garthwaite".

PORTEE A collection of threads warped together. The portees are mentioned by Leman because he was a manufacturer as well as a designer. Sometimes the portees are listed as numbers at the foot of a design. The actual number of threads in each portee is determined by the intended width of the warp and the total number of threads in it.

ROCAILLE A French term adopted to describe the stylised rocks which gave their name to the Rococo Style. These rocks were inspired by the fashionable artificial grottoes of the time and became a popular chinoiserie motif (see plate 81, 82).

RULE PAPER (R.P.) See POINT PAPER.

SATIN A weave and, by extension, a material. Satin is based on 5 or more warp threads and an equal number of shoots of weft. The points of binding never touch and are set over two or more threads on successive shoots. The meaning has not changed since the 18th century. As none of the points of binding touch one another the weave produces a smooth and apparently unbroken surface which reflects the light admirably and is therefore especially suitable for silks, glazed worsteds and linen damasks.

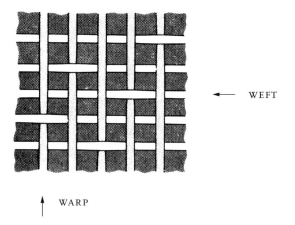

← WEFT

↑ WARP

SHADE The word was used by Garthwaite to mean a colour, any colour, not in the modern sense of a variety of one colour.

SHUTTLE A shuttle is the implement which the weaver uses to carry the weft across the material he is making. The word was used, however, in a much more technical sense by the designers, for it helps to denote the payments which would be necessary when the cloth was woven. In each pass there would have been a ground weft and one or more pattern or brocaded wefts. If the total number of all kinds of wefts in one repeat is divided by the total number of passes the result is the slightly odd fraction which is written on many of the designs e.g. "1 shuttle $\frac{1}{2}$ bro.", plate 112, or "$11\frac{1}{4}$", plate 116. As part of their wages the journeymen were paid a rate per shuttle up to a certain number and a slightly reduced rate above this, according to the 1769 List of Prices. The costs in Leman's day are unknown, but the master weaver needed to know the number of shuttles before he could calculate the labour costs and therefore whether it was practicable to market a design. (We are indebted to Mrs. Ulla Cyrus-Zetterstrom for elucidating this problem).

SIMPLE   The cords of a drawloom which are suspended vertically from the tail cords to the floor and to which the lashes are attached. When the length of the pattern warranted it, several simples could be attached to the tail cords. All the drawboy had to do was to move on from one set to the next when he had finished that section of the pattern. There does not seem to have been any fixed number of lashes before another simple was added.

TABBY   This is a plain weave classified by weight, i.e. more or less warp threads and wefts to the inch. The heavier tabbies were often slightly ribbed and could be watered (plate 130 could be treated thus), while paduasoys were heavier still. A double tabby was a heavy fabric, "double" because it had an extra binding warp, paradoxically binding the pattern in twill. They required "a grand look" according to the *Laboratory*. Leman's "paduasoy or tabby tissue", plate 15, would have been such a material.

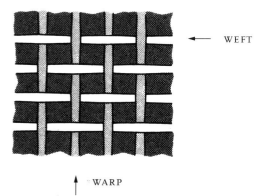

WEFT

WARP

TAFFETA   A plain weave but a much lighter fabric than tabby. The material was versatile and the meaning seems to have changed little since the 18th century.

TISSUE   Tissues had two warp and two weft systems and have been called by modern textile historians diasper and lampas (the current French term). The latter is defined by CIETA as a patterned textile with weft floats bound by a binding warp on a ground formed by a main warp and a main weft. In this period the pattern is bound in one weave, usually 3 & 1 twill, on a ground in another weave, such as tabby or satin or, more elaborately, on a damask or tobine ground. Tissues allowed the making of the complex effects which are the essence of 18th century silk design. The lace patterns of the 1720s are very often tissues, plates 24, 25, 26, etc., but the weave was much less relevant to the designs of the 1740s. The tissue was a material of specialised construction recognised by all those handling drawloom-woven materials: designers, draftsmen, master weavers, journeymen, mercers, and customers. It was intrinsically expensive, but James Leman economised by having looms already set up, for he states that a design is to be made in "the satin tissue harness", and by taking his binding warp from the ground or main warp. Garthwaite sometimes gives the effect of a more elaborate construction by using a pattern weft "in changes" – that is by changing the colour of the bobbin in the shuttle. This would give a superficial impression of several pattern wefts when in fact only one was used. With the invention of the jacquard mechanism the term and the material became obsolete.

TOBINES   These had an extra warp floating on the surface and bound at intervals. This either formed a background surface texture, as in plate 87, or the complete design. The colours can be varied across the warp, as in plate 101, and have additional weft effects. The length of the float was variable. The *Laboratory* described, p.41, "Lutestring tobines, which commonly are striped with flowers in the warp and sometimes between the stripes with brocaded sprigs. Some have likewise a running trail with the colour of the ground".

TRAINED BAND   A number of the weavers mentioned on the Garthwaite designs bear a military rank, "Capt. Peter Lekeux" for example. This they held in the Trained Bands of the City of London, a voluntary force raised for defence at home.

TWILL   A weave in which the points of binding of warp and weft are distributed so that in successive passes oblique parallel lines are formed. It is a much more supple weave than tabby and when used alone became much more important in the second half of the 18th century and the early 19th century, when materials were required to drape effectively. A minimum of three shafts are needed to make a twill, though many variations are possible. It was a weave much used for the binding of the patterns in tissues in the earlier part of the 18th century.

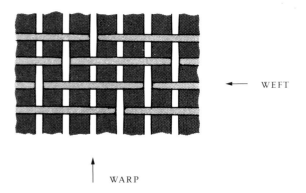

WEFT

WARP

VELVET   A pile fabric made by the warp and intrinsically the most expensive material on the market, both because of the quantity of silk used and because of the technique. A foundation warp had to bind the fabric and each pile warp thread was wound on its own bobbin. Weaving was very slow,

since wires had to be inserted under the pile warp at the correct intervals; some of the wires were grooved, allowing the pile warp to be cut with a special knife.

WARP   The threads entered in the loom before weaving. There may be several warps, each rolled on its separate warp beam. Their threads are entered in the heddles on shafts in a pre-determined sequence and on the drawloom are also controlled by the figure harness. They are raised as required for the passage of the weft.

WEAVER   See JOURNEYMAN WEAVER and MASTER WEAVER.

WEFT   The weft is carried on bobbins within shuttles and passed by the weaver across the warp or a section of the warp. There may be several different kinds of weft in one textile: ground, pattern or brocaded. They may be made of different materials to the warp. In most 18th century textiles it is the weft rather than the warp which makes the pattern. Exceptions are damask, relying on a contrast of light reflecting from warp and weft, and tobines, a purely warp effect. Wefts in patterned silks are thicker and glossier than the warp threads in the same material, which are more tightly twisted, for strength rather than beauty.

WORSTED   A wool, generally from a special breed of sheep, which is carded and then combed to give a smooth rather than a fluffy surface. It was often heavily glazed in the 18th and early 19th century and used extensively for high quality furnishings and costume.

BIOGRAPHICAL NOTES

ALEXANDER, MR. A mercer, probably James Alexander, of the firm of Alexander & Co. of Bedford Street, Covent Garden, active c.1702-22 and later.

BAKER, CAPTAIN JOHN A rich and distinguished silk weaver (1693-1783) and a considerable philanthropist, who made much of his money from the house property he owned and the ale-houses he possessed in and near Spitalfields, together with his investment in Truman & Hanbury's brewery. He was a member of the Flowered Branch of the industry, making the richest patterned materials. He bought 45 designs from Anna Maria Garthwaite, at least two of which have survived as silks. He was regularly apprenticed in the Weavers Company and had a long and active career, holding its highest office, Upper Bailiff, in 1743. He sat on many committees and gave evidence to Parliament about the industry several times. He was equally active in the local Vestry and offered 75 of his men to serve against the Young Pretender in 1745 – one of the highest offers (and according to his obituary drilled them himself). He lived well in Princes Street, mentioning his "coach and all other carriages" in his will.

BATCHELOR, HAM and PERIGAL The firm, whose pattern books became part of the Warner Archive, survived for over a century. The firm began with John Batchelor, apprenticed in 1694, and ended with the death of John Ham in the 1820s. Three generations of Batchelors can be traced before other partners took their place. After 1782 the firm became Harvey, Ham, and Perigal, then Jourdain and John Ham from 1793. The first partners were resident in Spital Square for many years before moving to White Lion Street, their address in Mortimer's Directory of 1763, when they advertised as weavers of gold and silver brocaded and flowered silk. The first Batchelor died in 1737; the second, a customer of Garthwaite, gave evidence to Parliament and had otherwise a notable career. The following pattern books from the firm were acquired by the Victoria and Albert Museum in 1972, T.374 to T.377 and T.382-1972.

BAUDOUIN, CHRISTOPHER c.1665-before 1736. Silk designer, by repute "the first that brought the flowered silk manufacture in credit and reputation here in England". According to a 19th century source he was one of the founders of the English silk industry with a group of silk weavers, Lanson, Marescoe and Monceaux. A number of Garthwaite's "Patterns by different hands" were by Baudouin – carried out for Captain Peter Lekeux (see below) whose uncle Peter had married the daughter of Peter Marescoe. Monceaux is also mentioned on these designs. Baudouin was resident in London by 1685, when a daughter was born to him; he was naturalised in 1709 and had died by 1736 when his widow made her own will. He lived in Paternoster Row and signed the Petition for the Building of one of the 50 New Churches as one of the "Principal Inhabitants" of Spitalfields.

BINCKES, MR. A mercer, George Binckes, died 1728, junior partner in the firm of Isaac Tullie (see below) established in Bedford Street, Covent Garden, at the King's Arms and Seven Stars. They supplied silks to the Crown, including those for the Funeral of George I and the Coronation of George II. The third partner, Henry Shelley, died in 1736.

BOOTH, MR. The name is a common one, but he can be tentatively identified with Daniel Booth senior, of Ropemakers Alley, Moorfields. He came from Canterbury and was admitted to the London Weavers Company as a Foreign Weaver in 1712. He had a long and active career, twice giving evidence to Parliament, and became Upper Bailiff of the Company in 1746. He retired to Hackney, then regarded as "the largest and most wealthy village in Europe remarkable for the number of opulent merchants..." where he died in 1764.

BRANT, THOMAS A silk weaver of Hand Alley off Bishopsgate Street, a Liveryman of the Weavers Company. His brother James was a throwster of some importance. Thomas offered 17 men to serve against the Young Pretender in 1745.

CARR, ROBERT 1707-91. The senior partner in one of the most important firms of mercers during the 18th century, which lasted with several changes of partnership from 1727, when it was founded by Ebenezer Ibbetson, until the early 19th century. They supplied goods to the Crown, both dress materials and furnishings, from the 1740s until the 1790s, when the firm were among the unpaid creditors of the Prince Regent. Apart from their premises, the Queen's Head on Ludgate Hill, acquired in 1731, they owned two other shops. Their fashionable customers included Mrs. Delany. They were importers of raw silk on their own account, suspected smugglers of foreign silks and thus the only firm to have its windows smashed during the crisis of 1765. They were customers of Garthwaite's chief weavers and at least thirty of her designs were commissioned by them. They gave evidence to Parliament in 1765. Carr himself retired to a country house at Hampton in Middlesex, but both Bigge and Ibbetson, whose names appear on the Batchelor Ham and Perigal books, were later partners. Samuel Ibbetson signed a bill on behalf of Ibbetson, Barlow and Clarke to the Prince Regent in 1792.

CHAPLIN, JOHN A master weaver, customer of Garthwaite in 1748-49, but little more is known about him.

DANDRIDGE, JOSEPH 1660-1746. Silk designer and naturalist who lived in Moorfields. He worked for James Leman (17 of his designs have survived) but achieved distinction as a botanist, ornithologist and entomologist and wrote two treatises now in the British Museum. He went on field expeditions in the time he could "spare from his business" and formed a scientific collection which was shown to and appreciated by scientific visitors. He was the master of John Vansommer, Garthwaite's contemporary and probable rival. His surviving designs are for the least naturalistic designs – those using metal thread.

GARTHWAITE, ANNA MARIA 1690-1763. Silk designer who worked freelance in Spitalfields from about 1730 until 1756. She came from a well-to-do clerical family; her father, who held several livings, resided in Grantham. Her twice-widowed elder sister married clergymen and between 1726 and 1728 Anna Maria lived with Mary "in York before I came to London". How she obtained the technical training necessary to design silks successfully is unknown. The sisters lived with their ward on the corner of Princes Street, surrounded by her customers. She produced over a thousand designs for the leading weavers and mercers of her day, on average about 80 designs per year. The designs for 1746 and most of 1750 are missing. Despite the stylistic reaction against rococo, her name remained a by-word in the industry, lingering as a trade-mark on a popular brand of point-paper until the 1830s.

GOBBÉ, DANIEL Before 1690-1758. Silk weaver and probable customer of Anna Maria Garthwaite. He was one of a large group of Huguenot emigrants from Bas-Poitou and was a loyal member both of the Weavers Company and the Vestry of Christ Church, Spitalfields. He made one of the largest offers of men to fight the Young Pretender – 70 men – and by 1749 was living in Princes Street. He gave evidence to Parliament in 1750, by which time he said he had been in trade for 45 years. He had exported silks to Ireland and his evidence confirmed him as a weaver of flowered silks.

GREGORY, MR. Although Garthwaite sold 40 designs to this weaver between 1742 and 1745 and the surviving silk woven from one of them is of the highest quality, it has proved impossible to identify him. The English community was less cohesive than the Huguenot and thus no references to a possible Gregory have appeared in material concerned with other English weavers.

HALSEY See PALMER & HALSEY

IBBETSON Ebenezer, Samuel and John Ibbetson were the partners of Robert Carr (see above). Ebenezer was the founder of the firm and the others may have been his sons or grandsons, for he retired in 1757.

JULINS, SIMON 1687/8-1774. Silk weaver. He became free of the Weavers Company in 1710 and subsequently a Liveryman. From 1728 until his death he lived in Booth Street, then a respectable but not a fashionable street. He offered 22 of his men to fight the Young Pretender in 1745. He bought several different kinds of design from Garthwaite between 1742 and 1755 and so far 9 silks woven by him have come to light, nearly all damasks. It was as a specialist in this one kind of flowered silk that he advertised in Mortimer's Directory of 1763. Most of his silks have survived in the chief markets to which English silks were exported, Scandinavia and the American Colonies, the most remarkable being the damask worn by Mrs. Charles Willing in her portrait by Robert Feke, painted in 1746; the silk was designed by Garthwaite in 1743.

LANDON, JOHN LUKE c.1705-56. Silk weaver. According to family tradition "the richest man in Norton Falgate". He was the son of a Huguenot who came to London via Rotterdam, settling in London about 1686. John Luke became a Liveryman in 1741 and offered 48 men to serve against the Young Pretender in 1745. He was among the first contributors to the London Hospital and Governor of the French Hospital in 1753. His sons and their cousins could also have been Garthwaite's customers, for all were weavers of flowered silks.

LARDANT, JAMES Before 1694-1761. Silk weaver, one of a large and extended Huguenot family from Normandy. They had been settled in England for some time, for unlike the Landons they had begun to marry English girls well before the mid 18th century and gave their children English names. Most of the Lardants, including his 9 surviving children, entered the silk industry, but were associated with plain materials. James was a Liveryman of the Weavers Company and offered 27 men to fight the Young Pretender in 1745. He lived in a house a few doors away from Garthwaite.

LEKEUX, CAPTAIN PETER 1684-1743. Silk weaver. His family, including his uncle, Colonel Peter, and son, Mr. Peter Lekeux, were active for over a century and among the richest and most important master weavers. Their careers in the Weavers Company, as witnesses giving evidence to Parliament and to the Commissioners for Trades and Plantations, indicate that they were very influential and the first Huguenots, together with James Leman, to be accepted by their English colleagues. To Colonel Lekeux was attributed the very foundation of the industry. Captain Peter was associated initially with Christopher Baudouin and later bought designs from Garthwaite. All the Lekeux made the finest and most expensive kinds of flowered silk, but came increasingly to specialise on the richest silks for men's wear. The mercers whom they supplied were, like Carr, firms with royal appointments.

LEMAN, JAMES c. 1688-1745, "The late ingenious Mr. Lemon", the only master weaver who was also a silk designer. His father Peter came to London from Amsterdam via Canterbury and James worked for him until Peter's death in 1713. Through the early designs the development of the bizarre style can be followed, while the later ones represent the transitional years before the fully developed lace patterns. Leman's designs have an added technical and historic interest because of their extensive inscriptions. He had an important career in the Weavers Company, took an active interest in the general well-being of the industry, and was a man of wide general interests. He disposed in his will of his "paintings, drawings...collection of prints, reading books, Musick, picture books and collection of copy books, musical and mathematical instruments..., collection of reptiles in spirits, collection of medals and coins..." while in his life time he subscribed to Eleazar Albin's books on Insects and Birds, in 1724 and 1738 respectively. Although he continued to be active in the industry, no designs have survived later than 1722.

MASE (OR MAZE) FAMILY The family came from Normandy and apart from one John Maze, who was a butcher, most entered the silk industry. Two parallel branches had each a pair of brothers James and John and since both married into the same Huguenot families they have proved impossible to disentangle. They achieved considerable prosperity as a clan, leaving substantial sums in their wills, in both real estate and funds.

PALMER & HALSEY Mercers, of the Blackamoor's Head, later 8, Ludgate Hill. The firm was founded by Miles Halsey about 1720 and he was at the address above by 1736. Philip Palmer joined forces with him in 1744. They bought 49 designs from Garthwaite between 1742 and 1749 which were woven by some of the leading weavers of flowered silks, four of whom gave evidence to Parliament on the condition of the silk industry in 1765. The majority of the designs which they bought were, however, woven by one weaver, Daniel Vautier, who only occasionally seems to have worked for any other mercer – at least when carrying out the Garthwaite designs. Halsey left the partnership in 1755 and his place was taken by Robert Fleetwood. Philip Palmer died or retired by 1760, but

Fleetwood and Palmer junior bought designs from another designer, P.A. de Brissac. Fleetwood gave evidence to Parliament in 1765 and 1766. They handled both English and foreign silks and showed some animosity towards the silk weavers who, they said, "treat the mercers as if they were their servants".

SABATIER, JOHN c.1702-80. A silk weaver from one of the rare Huguenot families from Lyon. He bought 90 designs from Garthwaite between 1742 and 1756, for many different kinds of silk. His eminence can be judged by the fact that on three occasions he submitted evidence to Select Committees of the House of Commons and on the last occasion, in 1766, he revealed some interesting biographical details. He had been going to the mercers for orders since 1721 and it was Sabatier who recalled 1748-50 as the best years which the industry had known. He mentioned that he had exported silks and from another source we know that he bought raw silk and had it thrown on his own account. According to his evidence he had had a large labour force, 400 at the most (at 4 men to a loom). He held a respected position in the community as an elder of the French Church and a Trustee or Commissioner under the local acts of 1753 and 1772. He retired to Chichester and his will gives a picture of a prosperous and likeable man.

TULLIE, ISAAC Active from 1693/4, died 1721. A mercer, senior partner of George Binckes and Henry Shelley at the Black Lion and Seven Stars on the west side of Bedford Street, Covent Garden. The firm had a succession of royal appointments and from Henry Shelley's inventory it is clear they stocked only the most expensive silks on the market, for both costume and furnishings. With the death of the third partner in 1736 the shop was sold.

VANSOMMER, JOHN 1705-74. Silk designer and partner in the firm of Ogier, Vansommer and Triquet of Spital Square. He was a neighbour of James Leman in Steward Street as a child and apprenticed to the designer and naturalist Joseph Dandridge. He became free of the Merchant Taylors Company in 1727 and was thus still a young man when credited by Postlethwayt with being one of three designers to introduce the principles of painting into the loom. He had a successful career and was a respected member of the community, becoming a Trustee under the Local Act of 1759. He became a correspondent of Voltaire which suggests a man of wide intellectual attainment. The one surviving silk designed by him has come down in the family into which his eldest daughter married.

VAUTIER, DANIEL c.1696-probably 1760. Silk weaver of Steward Street and later Lamb Street, Spitalfields. He was a Liveryman of the Weavers Company and offered 47 men to serve against the Young Pretender. Although there are a number of Vautiers in the industry the genealogical evidence suggests that this man was Garthwaite's chief customer, buying 106 designs for many different kinds of silk between 1741 and 1751, from which at least five silks have survived.

WRIGHT, MRS. PHOEBE Silk designer and embroideress. In 1751 Postlethwayt mentions her among a small group of silk designers who had become prominent since 1744, commenting on the "correctness and elegancy of her drawing and colouring". Mrs. Delany mentions a dress embroidered by Mrs. Wright in 1742 in "gold and colours on white". She was described as "a pattern drawer of eminence" to the 1765 Select Committee of the House of Commons on the silk industry. Her later career seems to have been exclusively as an embroideress as she had a royal appointment to Queen Charlotte. By comparison with a set of embroideries in a private collection one silk has been tentatively attributed to her.